SWEET + SWISS

DELICIOUS & EASY DESSERTS
FROM THE HEART OF EUROPE

HEDDI NIEUWSMA
DORIAN ROLLIN

SWEET + SWISS

DELICIOUS AND EASY DESSERTS FROM THE HEART OF EUROPE

TABLE OF CONTENTS

I

INTRODUCTION
EINFÜHRUNG
INTRODUCTION

I. INTRODUCTION

What makes sweet recipes from Switzerland so special?

From crisp hazelnut biscuits to a 'burnt cream' pudding to rich chocolate tarts with an unexpected green icing, Switzerland has an irresistible collection of sweet recipes. When I moved here in 2012 from the United States, it gave me the chance to discover a completely new food scene. I began cooking with ingredients I had never used before. For sweet dishes, this meant ingredients such as absinthe, caraway seeds, and spiced sandalwood sugar.

Despite being roughly twice the size of New Jersey, Switzerland has a diverse culinary heritage. You can enjoy a rustic alpine dessert in the mountains, such as the Schlorzifladen (p. 129), or a delicate citrus soufflé from one of the finest restaurants in the world. The country has few national dishes, but certain sweet recipes are well known by almost everyone. The Spitzbuben, for example, a jammy sandwich cookie (p. 173) that goes by several other names, or a box of crisp meringues (p. 213) can be found in many parts of the country. At the same time, Switzerland's four linguistic regions—German, French, Italian and Romansh—have a number of deeply rooted sweet treats that do not always transcend their borders.

Even within these linguistic regions, certain sweet dishes really only exist in their canton (similar to states) or even their village of origin. A yeasted bread with raisins called Pitta from Graubünden (p. 23), or a fruit tart known as the Flon de Savièse from Valais (p. 115), are perfect examples. Numerous recipes have connections to local celebrations or holidays. In the Jura, for instance, you might have a refreshing plum sorbet as part of the Feast of St. Martin. In Ticino, bakers make Pane dei morti (p. 73) in the fall around the time of All Saints' Day (November 1) and Day of the Dead (All Souls' Day on November 2). For such a small country, these regional specialties and the stories behind them continue to fascinate and inspire me to learn more.

How did I develop these sweet recipes?

This book brings together a selection of my favorite sweet recipes for some traditionally Swiss dishes. You may have noticed that in my first book, *Swiss Bread* (2020), the chapter titled *Sweet Breads and Yeasted Cakes* has the most recipes. Given my affinity for desserts, both for making and tasting them, it should not surprise anyone that I chose to focus entirely on sweet recipes for my second book.
Here you will find 45 recipes for traditional breads, pastries, cakes, cookies and creamy desserts from Switzerland.

These recipes, all based on existing Swiss dishes, come from years of research and reflection since I arrived in Switzerland. In 2015, I started my blog about Swiss food, drink and culinary travel, naming it *Cuisine Helvetica*. Via this online space, I share what I learn about uniquely Swiss ingredients and traditional dishes. My articles feature recipes, interviews with chefs, information about culinary events and more. I enjoy connecting with people all over the world to help broaden awareness of Swiss food—beyond the image of chocolate and cheese.

Through my blog, I have had wonderful opportunities to visit many corners of Switzerland. Whenever I board a Swiss train to another stunning destination, I search for specialties at local bakeries. I go to public libraries in these communities to leaf through the pages of old cookbooks. I reach out to museums, bakery associations, restaurants and tourism offices. People who have grown up in Switzerland or Swiss who live abroad share their stories with me, so I can record their experiences and memories tied to a particular recipe.

Over the years, I have tried a myriad of different recipes for these dishes to see which methods work best for home cooks—and which have the best taste. They come from all across Switzerland. Some recipes can be thrown together quickly, such as the Lebkuchen (p. 79), while others require more time and patience, like the little hazelnut-meringue cakes from Solothurn (p. 133). I tested and retested these recipes, with the support of generous volunteers, so that you can recreate these sweet dishes yourself at home.

Which restaurant recipes appear in this book?

For this book, I selected five restaurants to visit and write about, covering all of Switzerland's linguistic regions. The chefs at each of these restaurants gave me permission to include one of their recipes in this book! These five recipes reflect the regions where their restaurants are located and the individual experiences of these talented chefs. You will read about an innovative plant-based restaurant in Zürich, a charming hotel restaurant in a mountain village, a historic chalet in rural French-speaking Switzerland, a Michelin-starred restaurant near St. Gallen and an island grotto in the middle of the Ticino River. Each restaurant has their own unique story, but they all have a strong commitment to using local ingredients and showcasing regional Swiss cuisine.

As I like to say, you can learn a lot about Switzerland's history, culture and geography through its food. Thankfully, this also applies to its sweet breads, cakes, tarts, cookies and more! It's a delicious way to discover this incredible little country that I now call home. I hope these Swiss-inspired recipes will bring you joy and the stories that accompany them will inspire you to explore its beautiful landscapes.

Stay sweet,
Heddi Nieuwsma

Schlossgut Münchenwiler, located in Münchenwiler (Bern), Switzerland, and managed by Stiftung Ferien im Baudenkmal, served as the location for our photo shoot. For more information, please see p. 230.

P.S. Please tag your #SweetSwissBook photos. It makes me so happy to see what you are making, and we can learn much from each other. I will gladly repost my favorites via social media:

@CUISINEHELVETICA

@CUISINEHELVETICA

@HEDDI_ELISE

SWEET RECIPES FROM FIVE SWISS RESTAURANTS

RESTAURANT KLE, P. 105
Zweierstrasse 114
8003 Zürich

AUBERGE DU CHALET-DES-ENFANTS, P. 137
Rte du Chalet-des-Enfants
1052 Le Mont-sur-Lausanne

NEUE BLUMENAU, P. 199
Romanshornerstrasse 2
9308 Lömmenschwil

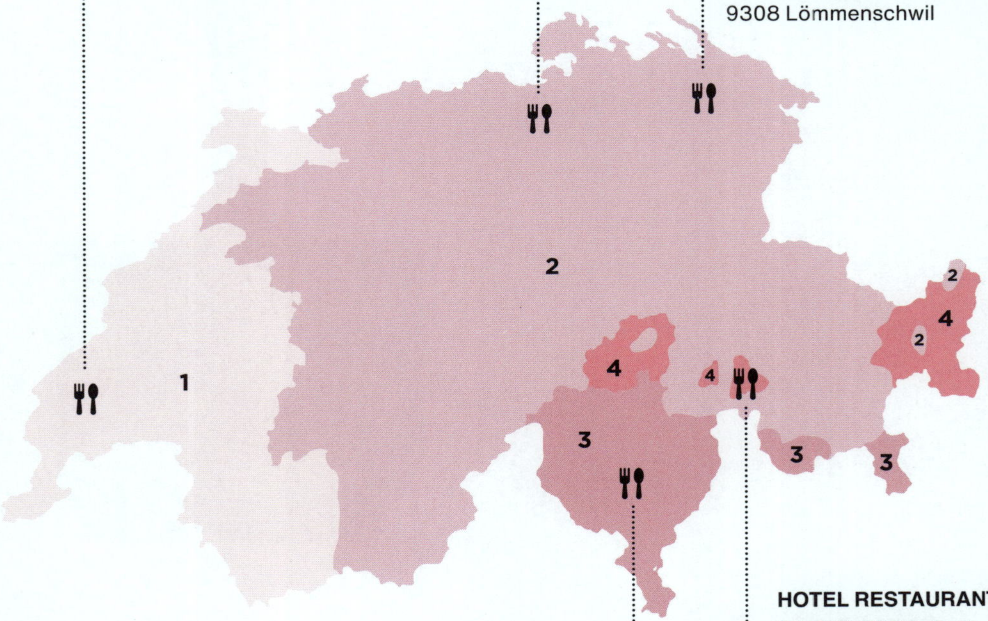

HOTEL RESTAURANT CAPRICORNS, P. 61
Veia Cantunala 51
7433 Casti-Wergenstein

GROTTO DEI DUE PONTI, P. 83
Via ai Pontini 11
6745 Giornico

1 **FRENCH**

2 **GERMAN**

3 **ITALIAN**

4 **ROMANSH**

Source for the four language regions of Switzerland by Municipality:
Federal Statistical Office, Geospatial Division of Switzerland, 2020

II

BACKGROUND
GRUNDSÄTZLICHES
POUR COMMENCER

To the extent it might be helpful, here are some notes about a selection of ingredients and tools that I use for the recipes in this book.

A. MEASURING INGREDIENTS

All the recipes in the book have measurements by weight (grams) and volume (cups, teaspoons and tablespoons). I grew up learning to bake in the United States with measuring cups and spoons. Since moving to Switzerland, I have transitioned to using a kitchen scale that measures my ingredients by weight. While this book contains both types of measurements, weighing your ingredients will give you the most accurate results.

KEY INGREDIENTS

Flour / Mehl / Farine / Farina

Flour can be very different, depending on whether you buy it at a supermarket or a small flour mill. Also, each country seems to have its own nomenclature for classifying flour types. Even the time of year can affect your baking with flour, as humidity levels can increase during the summer months and decrease during the colder winter months.

To reduce challenges with finding flour substitutions if you do not live in Switzerland, I decided to develop recipes with what might be considered more commonly used flours. As a result, the recipes in this book call for basics like 'all-purpose flour' or 'whole wheat flour'. Here is a profile of these flours, in case you are looking for substitutions where you live and bake.

SWISS FLOUR TYPE	IN FRANCE	IN GERMANY	IN THE US
White flour (type 550) Weissmehl (DE) farine blanche / farine fleur (FR) farina bianca (IT) Degree of grinding: 0-65% Protein content: 12%	farine blanche (T55)	Weissmehl (type 550)	all-purpose flour OR bread flour for the yeasted recipes in the first chapter
Whole wheat flour (type 1900) Vollkornmehl (DE) farine complète (FR) farina integrale (IT) Degree of grinding: 98-100% Protein content: 14%	farine complète OR farine intégrale (T150)	Vollkornmehl	whole wheat flour

In the United States, for example, a likely substitute for white flour would be 'all-purpose flour' for cakes and cookies. For the breads in Chapter I, however, I would recommend using a flour with a higher protein content. Conveniently, these bags are often labeled as 'bread flour.' In the United Kingdom a 'plain flour' might be suitable for cakes and cookies, while a 'strong white flour' would be better for breads.

When converting flour from grams to cups, I noticed that this ratio differs greatly among American bakers. I found authors and bloggers using a range of different amounts, varying from about 120 to 142 grams, for one cup of flour. This can have a big impact on your experience using a particular recipe!

Based on my tests at home here in Switzerland, and among my recipe testers in the United States and the United Kingdom, I have decided to use a ratio of 125 grams per one cup of all-purpose flour for the recipes in this book. This ratio requires that you use the traditional spoon-and-level method. First, you aerate the flour in its container by stirring it with a spoon. Then, you spoon the flour into a measuring cup. Once the cup is overflowing with flour, you level it off.

Please note: If your measuring cup at home yields a weight that differs from 125 grams of flour, you may need to increase or decrease the amount of flour you use for my recipes.

Oven / Backofen / Four / Forno

Unless otherwise stated, nearly all the recipes in this book indicate baking temperatures for a conventional oven with top / bottom heat. If you have a convection oven, you will have to make adjustments to the baking time or temperature for these recipes.

Milk / Milch / Lait / Latte

When a recipe calls for milk, I generally use milk with 2.5% milk fat. In some cases, where specified, I use what can be described as 'whole milk' (3.5% milk fat).

Butter / Butter / Beurre / Burro

Unsalted butter is the norm for baking in Switzerland. As such, all the recipes in this book that call for 'butter' refer to unsalted butter. If you normally cook or bake with butter that contains salt, then you may want to reduce the amount of salt added to the recipe.

The Swiss unsalted butter that I usually use has 82 percent butterfat. It also typically contains bacteria that encourage the development of lactic acid. This process of fermentation occurs before the butter is churned. In the United States, if possible, I recommend using a European-style butter with this higher fat content. This particularly applies to recipes with a large proportion of butter, such as pastry dough for tarts. These butters are said to have a richer and tangier flavor, in comparison to American butters, as well as a deeper yellow color.

Yeast / Hefe / Levure / Lievito

For all the recipes in Chapter 3 that call for yeast, I use fresh organic yeast—sometimes referred to as cake yeast. A number of recipes also give the measurements for dry yeast, which has a longer shelf life. Generally, you can calculate the amount of dry yeast to use by dividing the amount of fresh yeast in a recipe by three.

When you use dry yeast, make sure to read the package to know what kind you have and how to use it. Some of these yeasts need to be activated in lukewarm water and other 'instant' yeasts can be added directly with flour and other ingredients. I prefer to dissolve whatever yeast I am using in lukewarm liquid first to help ensure that it is well distributed in the dough.

One of the most important things when using yeast is that you do not overheat the liquid you add it to. I always test the liquid first by touching it with my fingers. It should be at or just slightly warmer than body temperature.

Eggs / Eier / Œufs / Uova

In Switzerland, unless otherwise specified in the individual recipes, I generally use large eggs with a weight of about 63 grams (about 2 ¼ ounces) for the recipes in the book. In the United States, these eggs would generally be considered 'extra-large' in terms of their size. If you use an egg that is not within an average size of about 55-65 grams (about 2 to 2 ¼ ounces), then you may need to make adjustments to the recipe.

B. MY FAVORITE KITCHEN TOOLS FOR SWEET RECIPES

Plastic bowl scraper

Bench scraper

Whisk

Immersion blender

Electric mixer (upright mixer)

Dough thickness sticks (*teighölzi*)

Mixing bowls

Rubber scraper (spatula)

Reusable piping bag and piping tips

Baking sheet or cookie sheet

Parchment paper

Rolling pin

Saucepan

Frying pan

Muffin tin

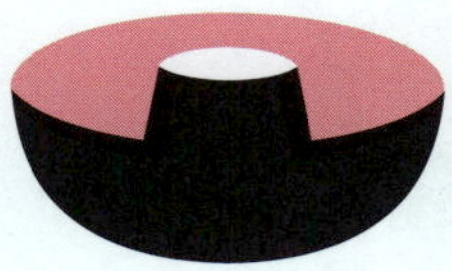

Bundt (Gugelhopf) pan

Springform pan

Pastry rings

Cookie cutters

Pastry dough blender

Wiler (Lötschen), bakery

Inspired by a late 19th to 20th century photo from the Verein Schweizerischer Geographielehrer; held by the Swiss National Library.

III

BREAD, YEASTED CAKES & PASTRIES

BROT, HEFEKUCHEN UND GEBÄCK

PAINS, GÂTEAUX LEVÉS ET VIENNOISERIES

III. BREAD, YEASTED CAKES & PASTRIES

This chapter features some of my favorite fluffy Swiss regional breads, yeasted cakes and pastries. I love a sweet slice of bread generously slathered with butter. The recipe for Einback (p.27), with just a touch of honey in the dough, is perfect for this, especially to start out your day. Throughout the morning, I also like to reach for a spiced fruit or nut-filled pastry with a hot cup of milky coffee. You can really eat these types of pastries any time—for breakfast or brunch, after a light meal or for an afternoon snack.

The Rosinenkranz (p. 23), for example, a bread wreath found in Nidwalden, relies on dried currants for its sweetness with no added sugar. In contrast, the Merishauser Bienenstich (p. 57), Switzerland's own version of the 'beesting' cake from the canton of Schaffhausen, has three sweet layers with a crunchy honey-hazelnut lid. Also, you may be surprised to see a yeasted cake from Vaud known as the Salée (salty) ormonanche (p. 53) in this chapter. Its savory name belies this cake's sweet cinnamon topping.

These comforting Swiss breads and pastries, for the most part, are meant to be eaten with your hands. Many of them are best served while still a bit warm and always to be shared with friends and family. Or you can keep them all for yourself and throw them in your freezer for another time.

1 ROSINENKRANZ

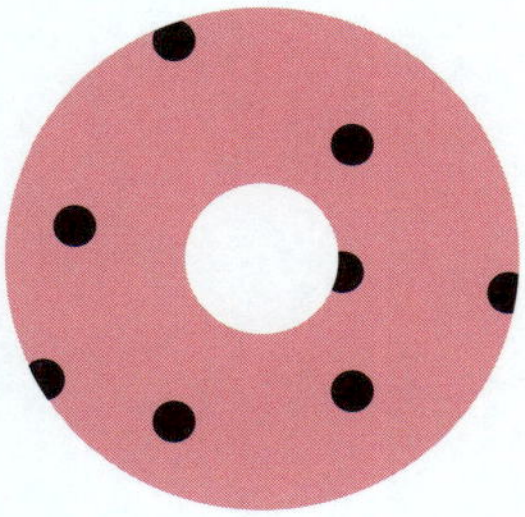

Preparation Time

approx. 3 hours 30 minutes
bake for 25-35 minutes

Quantity

Makes 1 round ring loaf.

INGREDIENTS

Dough

- 500 g (3 ½ to 4 cups) all-purpose or bread flour
- 6 g (1 teaspoon) salt
- 50 g (3 ½ tablespoons) unsalted butter, softened
- 1 egg, lightly beaten
- 10 g fresh yeast, crumbled (or 3.5 g / 1 ⅛ teaspoons dry yeast)
- 280 ml (1 cup + 3 tablespoons) milk, lukewarm
- 75 g (½ cup) dried currants

Brush on top:

- 1 egg, beaten

INSTRUCTIONS

1. In a large bowl, whisk the dry ingredients together: start with 500 g (or start with 3 ½ cups) of flour and the salt. Add the softened butter in pieces to the bowl, but do not mix it in. Then, make a well in the center of the mixture and add the slightly beaten egg. Set aside.

2. Add the yeast to the lukewarm milk and let it sit for a few minutes. Stir until the yeast has fully dissolved. Pour it into the center of the flour mixture in the large bowl with the other ingredients and stir together to form a dough. On a lightly floured surface, knead the dough for about 8 minutes by hand, or use an electric mixer with a dough hook. Add additional flour as needed, one tablespoon at a time, if the dough is too wet and sticky.

   During the last 1-2 minutes of kneading, when the dough starts to become smooth and elastic, add the dried currants to the dough. Knead the dough by hand until they become evenly distributed.

3. Place the dough in a bowl covered with a damp kitchen towel and let it rise for about 2-3 hours, until it has doubled in size.

4. Punch down the dough and gently shape into a round loaf. Make a hole in the center of the loaf, and carefully form it into a large dough-nut shape, with a diameter of approximately 23-25 cm (9-10 inches). Place on a baking sheet lined with parchment paper. Cover the dough loosely with a clean kitchen towel and let it rest for about 30 minutes.

5. Brush the beaten egg on the surface of the bread. Using a lame or sharp knife, make a circular cut in the middle and around the loaf on its surface, as shown in the image below. Next, take kitchen shears and make small diagonal cuts around the circle you just cut into the dough.

6. Bake the loaf at 200°C / 400°F for about 25-35 minutes, until it becomes golden brown on its surface. Place on a wire rack to cool.

A GENTLY SWEET BREAD CROWN FOR THE CHRISTMAS SEASON

I first encountered the Rosinenkranz in *Unser täglich Brot in der Geschichte und im Volksbrauch* ('Our Daily Bread in History and Popular Customs'). This book by Swiss bread researcher Max Währen was first published in 1951. I found it at the Richemont Craft School for the bakery and confectionery trade in Luzern. The photograph of this round bread with a hole in its middle appears on the page about loaves from the Swiss canton of Nidwalden. According to Währen, people had been baking Rosinenringe (another name for this bread) for at least 100 years in this canton, if not more.

The name of this bread implies that it contains raisins (Rosinen). However, the type of raisins used for this bread are called *korinthen* in German, *raisins de corinthe* in French or *uva secca del corinto* in Italian. Corinth, of course, refers to the city in Greece. Sometimes these are also known as Zante currants, in reference to the Greek Island where they are grown. In American English, we call them 'dried currants,' even though they are small, seedless grapes typically grown in the Mediterranean—not the small red or black berries that we typically refer to as currants. One story goes that in the early 20th century, when a shipment of these dried grapes arrived from Greece to the United States, a bad translation of 'Corinth,' written on the outside of the box, led to them being called dried currants.

Studded with these dried currants, the Rosinenkranz is essentially the Christmas version of the Rosinenweggen, an elongated oval loaf with these same diagonal slash marks, which you will also find in Nidwalden. Made with scissors, these slash marks also remind me of those on the surface of the Taillaule neuchâteloise—a Swiss bread from the canton of Neuchâtel often made with raisins.

My recipe for the Rosinenkranz does not contain any added sugar. It relies on the sweetness of the dried currants. This way, you can serve it with butter and honey or jam, as easily as you can with a slice of cheese. It has become one of my favorite Swiss breads—an impressive-looking loaf for the holiday season or any time of year.

2 EINBACK / ZWIEBACK

Preparation Time
approx. 3 hours 30 minutes (direct method)
or 18 hours (indirect method)
bake for 25-35 minutes

Quantity
Makes 1-2 loaves of bread.

INGREDIENTS

Poolish:*

- 1 g (a small pinch of) fresh yeast
- 100 g (¾ cup) all-purpose or bread flour
- 100 ml (¼ cup + 3 tablespoons) water, cold

Dough:

- 400 g (2 ¾ to 3 ¼ cups) all-purpose or bread flour
- 6 g (1 teaspoon) salt
- 60 g (4 tablespoons) unsalted butter, softened
- 42 g (2 tablespoons) honey
- 1 egg, lightly beaten
- 9 g (about ⅓ oz) fresh yeast, crumbled
- 150 ml (⅔ cup) milk, lukewarm

***Direct method:**

If you don't have fresh yeast or want to shorten the rising time, then skip the instructions for making a poolish. Instead, dissolve 7 grams (2 ¼ teaspoons) of active dry yeast in 100 ml (¼ cup + 3 tablespoons) lukewarm water. Then, add this mixture to the total amount of flour (500 g / 3 ½ to 4 cups) and all the remaining ingredients for the dough, as described in step 2 below.

Brush on before baking:

- 1 egg, beaten

INSTRUCTIONS

1. **Indirect method:** Prepare the poolish. In a small bowl, dissolve the fresh yeast in the cold water. Then, stir in the flour to make a wet, thick batter. Cover the bowl and let sit at room temperature for about 15-18 hours.

2. When the poolish is ready, make the dough. In a large bowl, whisk 400 g (or start with 2 ¾ cups of flour) and the salt together. Add the butter, in pieces, to the bowl, but do not mix it in. Then, make a well in the center of the mixture and add the honey and lightly beaten egg. Set aside.

3. Add the fresh yeast to the lukewarm milk. Let it sit for a few minutes and then stir together until the yeast has dissolved. Next, add the poolish and yeast mixture into the center of the large bowl. Stir until a dough forms.

4. On a lightly floured surface, knead the dough by hand for about 10 minutes, or use an electric mixer with a dough hook, until it becomes smooth and elastic. Add additional flour as needed, one tablespoon at a time, if the dough is too wet and sticky. Place the dough in a large bowl and cover it with a damp kitchen towel. Let the dough rise for about 1-2 hours, until it has doubled in size.

5. After the dough has risen, grease and flour two loaf pans, about 10 x 20 cm (4 x 8 ½ inches) or line them with parchment paper (you can also make this in a single larger loaf pan, but you may need to adjust the cooking time). Next, divide the dough in half. Take one half of the dough and cut it into seven equally sized pieces. Form each piece into an oblong shape, about the width of the loaf pan you're using. Place them in a row in the pan. Repeat with the other half of the dough in the second loaf pan. Cover both pans with a damp kitchen towel and let them rise for about 60 minutes.

6. After the second rise in the pan, remove the kitchen towel and brush the tops of the dough loaves lightly with a beaten egg.

7. For two loaves, bake for about 25-35 minutes at 180°C / 350°F, until the tops of the loaves have turned golden brown (for a single larger loaf, depending on the size of your pan, you may need to increase the baking time to 30-40 minutes). Take the bread out of the oven and let it cool in the pan for about 10 minutes. Then place the bread on a wire rack to cool.

Zwieback

To make Zwieback, slice the loaves about 24 hours after they have been baked, into pieces about 8 mm thick (⅓ of an inch). Place them on a baking sheet lined with parchment paper and bake them for about 25-30 minutes at 140°C / 275°F until they become crisp and very lightly browned around the edges.

ONCE- OR TWICE-BAKED BREAD SLICES

This recipe includes two phases. It starts with Einback, a fluffy brioche-style bread made with milk, butter and often eggs. You form this dough into a segmented loaf in a rectangular pan. Its name means 'once-baked' in German. This soft, irresistible loaf is the kind you can pull apart (or slice) and slather with lots of butter and perhaps a sweet spread. The (optional) second phase takes place when you slice this loaf and bake these slices into Zwieback (literally 'twice-baked'), which become crisp little toasts.

Before moving to Switzerland, I had never heard of Einback before, but I was familiar with Zwieback. My experience with Zwieback was as a teething biscuit for babies. I would not typically buy it (perhaps twice when my boys were infants), and it certainly was not something I made at home. Nor had I ever considered the meaning behind its name.

My recipe contains a small amount of honey, to give the Einback a slight sweetness. I also use an indirect method to make this bread. It requires a poolish, a pre-dough (or pre-ferment) made with a tiny amount of fresh yeast. I like using this method because it decreases the amount of yeast you need to use and increases the period of fermentation for the dough. In my opinion, this process helps to add greater flavor and texture to the bread. If you would prefer to use the direct method, or if you don't have easy access to fresh yeast, you can skip the step of making a poolish (you'll find instructions in the recipe).

Once you have baked your Einback loaf or loaves and 24 hours have passed, you can start making Zwieback. *Zwei* means *two* in German, but the prefix *zwi* means *twice* in Old High German. Baking slices of Einback at a low temperature reduces the humidity in the bread and makes them crisp. This process also helps to preserve the bread for longer.

Zwieback in Switzerland has the reputation as a snack for the sick. With a mild taste and a texture, these biscuits can help to soothe an upset stomach when you don't have much of an appetite. (The American equivalent, from my experience, would be saltine crackers.) Furthermore, industrial Zwieback is often fortified, with the addition of vitamin B and iron.

Research by Patrimoine Culinaire Suisse indicates that Zwieback has a history stretching back to the 16th century. Joseph Hug-Meyer is credited with inventing a more modern version of the Zwieback in central Switzerland in 1877. A few decades later in Graubünden, Joseph Laim received a patent for "Neuartige Zwiebackschnitten" (novelty Zwieback slices) in 1896. These biscuits were produced in Surava, and the Swiss army was an early customer. More than a century later, you can still find Laim's Castel Zwieback, made with the original recipe, at the Attenhofer bakery in Thusis.

In Switzerland, the majority of Zwieback sold to consumers today comes from industrial producers, rather than small artisanal bakeries. This movement occurred during the 20th century. A 1944 manual for the bakery and pastry sector in Switzerland contains no fewer than five different recipes for Zwieback, which hints at their previous importance to this sector. This book also devotes a rather significant portion of text to describing the value of making Zwieback, while highlighting the growing competition for this product from larger factories.

Today, as always, Zwieback are appreciated for their ability to stay fresh for a long time. During the Covid-19 pandemic, HUG, a large producer of Zwieback in central Switzerland, told a local newspaper in 2021 about the growth in sales of this product, once again appreciated for its shelf life. On their website, this company also describes how Zwieback are enjoyed by single people, and particularly young men. It states that unopened or well-packaged Zwieback can last for over a year!

A 2021 article in *Bilan*, a French-language business magazine based in Geneva, described Zwieback as the *madeleine de Proust* for Switzerland. This popular expression references the French novelist's description of how a little madeleine triggered a fond childhood memory. If you grew up in Switzerland, perhaps you also enjoyed this sweet rusk as an ingredient in a classic Swiss dessert known as Götterspeise ('food of the gods'). This layered dish is typically composed of Zwieback, fruit compote and vanilla cream (I have a recipe on my blog).

Whether you like the soft slices of Einback or the crispy Zwieback—you don't need to be sick to enjoy them—they are both part of the Swiss culinary tradition.

3 PITTA

Preparation Time
approx. 10-12 hours
bake for 25-30 minutes

Quantity
Makes about 12 bread muffins.

INGREDIENTS

Dough:

- 500 g (3 ½ to 4 cups) all-purpose or bread flour
- 40 g (3 tablespoons) sugar
- 6 g (1 teaspoon) salt
- 75 g (⅓ cup) unsalted butter, softened
- zest of one organic orange
- 2 eggs, lightly beaten
- 50 ml (¼ cup) freshly squeezed orange juice
- 1 teaspoon vanilla extract or paste
- 10 g fresh yeast, crumbled (or 3 ½ g / 1 ⅛ teaspoons dry yeast)
- 150 ml (⅔ cup) milk, lukewarm
- 75 g (½ cup) raisins

Toppings:

- 1 egg, beaten
- slivered almonds
- pearl sugar

INSTRUCTIONS

1. In a large bowl, whisk the dry ingredients together: start with 500 g (or start with 3 ½ cups) of flour, the sugar and the salt. Add the softened butter in pieces to the bowl, along with the orange zest, but do not mix it in. Then, make a well in the center of the mixture and add the eggs, orange juice and vanilla. Set aside.

2. Add the fresh yeast to the lukewarm milk. Let it sit for a few minutes and then stir until the yeast has dissolved.

3. Pour the yeast mixture into the middle of the flour mixture in the large bowl. Stir until a dough forms.

4. Knead the dough for approximately 10 minutes by hand, or with an electric mixer with a dough hook, until it becomes smooth and elastic. Add additional flour as needed, one tablespoon at a time, if the dough is too wet and sticky. When the dough is almost ready, knead in the raisins by hand until they are evenly distributed.

5. Place the dough in a bowl covered with a damp kitchen towel. Let it rise for about 2-3 hours or until it has doubled in size.

6. Grease a muffin tin with butter. Divide the dough into twelve equal pieces. Form each of the pieces into round buns and place them in the muffin tin. Cover them loosely with a damp kitchen towel and place in the fridge overnight.

7. In the morning, take the bread muffins out of the fridge, keep them covered and let them sit at room temperature for about 1-2 hours. Then, brush the surface of the rolls with the beaten egg and sprinkle with the slivered almonds and pearl sugar.

8. Bake them for about 25-30 minutes on the bottom rack of the oven at 180˚C / 350˚F until their surface becomes golden brown. Place them on a wire rack to cool. Serve warm with butter.

ELECTION DAY BREAD FROM THE SCHANFIGG DISTRICT OF GRAUBÜNDEN

Pitta is a yeasted cake containing raisins typically eaten during the celebrations of the New Year in the canton of Graubünden. More specifically, this specialty comes from the Mittelbünden region, or the central part of the canton, and particularly the town of Thusis. *Petta* means 'cake' in Romansh, which seems the likely origin of its name. You could describe this cake as the regional cousin of Bütschella, a little bread bun also made with raisins found in Graubünden's Engadin Valley.

Once reserved for the holiday season, Pitta can now be purchased throughout the year at bakeries like Widmer in Arosa. The owner, Jörg Widmer, told me that this sweet bread was traditionally made for the Bsatzig. This local festival used to take place about every two or three years in the mountain village of St. Peter for the entire Schanfigg district. Historically, this get-together occurred for the purpose of holding local elections, with the celebration taking place after the official proceedings. Once the election was over, everyone would feast on local specialties, such as boiled ham, *bindenfleisch* (another name for *bündnerfleisch*, a dried beef), Pitta and wine. This outdoor election first began in 1851 and continued up until 2009. After a decade's long absence, a special Schanfigger Bsatzigspüntel event took place in 2019 to celebrate this historical tradition, which included a workshop on how to make your own Pitta at home.

I have seen Pitta sprinkled with either sliced or slivered almonds. For my recipe, I was inspired by a version of the Pitta from the Widmer's bakery, which uses slivered almonds. Instead of a larger, round cake, I shape the dough into little rolls and bake them in a muffin tin. When you start the dough overnight, you can bake them in the morning for breakfast or brunch. These sweet, satisfying little breads taste best when they're still warm and smeared with butter. Perhaps you might want to make them your own election day tradition?

The mountain village of St. Peter in Graubünden

4 NUSSGIPFEL

Preparation Time
approx. 2 hours 30 minutes
bake for 20-25 minutes

Quantity
Makes 6 crescent rolls.

INGREDIENTS

Dough:

- 175 g (1 ¼ to 1 ½ cups) all-purpose or bread flour
- 75 g (about ¾ cup) spelt flour
- ½ teaspoon salt
- 30 g (2 tablespoons) unsalted butter, softened
- 1 tablespoon honey
- ½ teaspoon vanilla extract or paste
- 10 g (⅓ oz) fresh yeast, crumbled (or 3 ½ g / 1 ⅛ teaspoons dry yeast)
- 125 ml (½ cup) milk, lukewarm

Filling:

- 160 g (2 cups) ground hazelnuts
- 42 g (2 tablespoons) honey
- 50 ml (about ¼ cup) milk
- 25 g (2 tablespoons) sugar
- zest of one organic orange
- 1 teaspoon cinnamon
- ¼ teaspoon nutmeg

INSTRUCTIONS

1. Make the dough. Whisk together 175 g (or start with 1 ¼ cups) of all-purpose or bread flour with the spelt flour and salt in a large bowl. Add the softened butter in pieces, but do not mix it in. Make a well in the center of the mixture and add the honey and vanilla. Set aside.

2. Add the yeast to the lukewarm milk. Let it sit for a few minutes and then stir until the yeast has dissolved.

3. Pour the yeast mixture into the center of the large bowl with all the other dough ingredients. Stir until a dough forms. Knead the dough on a lightly floured surface for about 10 minutes by hand, or use an electric mixer with a dough hook, until it becomes smooth and elastic. Add additional flour as needed, one tablespoon at a time, if the dough is too wet and sticky.

4. Place the dough in a bowl covered with a damp kitchen towel and let it rise for about 1-2 hours or until it doubles in size.

5. While the dough is rising, prepare the filling. Add all the ingredients into a bowl and stir until well combined.

6. When the dough is ready, place it on a lightly floured surface. Using a rolling pin lightly dusted with flour, roll out the dough into a flat, round circle with a diameter of approximately 28-30 cm (11-12 inches). Cut the dough into six triangles. If necessary, roll out each triangle again with a rolling pin so it's about 2-3 mm (1⁄10 of an inch) thick. Place a portion of the filling in the middle of the wide end of the triangle, and roll it up into a crescent-shaped roll, turning the points of the roll inward to create a curved shape. Place the roll on a baking sheet lined with parchment paper. Repeat with the remaining five portions of dough.

7. Cover the rolls loosely with a clean kitchen towel and let them rest for about 30 minutes.

8. Brush the crescent rolls lightly with the beaten egg. Then, bake for about 18-25 minutes at 200°C / 400°F until they become golden brown. Cool on a wire rack.

CRESCENT ROLLS WITH A SWEET NUT FILLING

Growing up in the United States, my experience with crescent rolls involved a cardboard cylinder with aluminum discs on either end. You can purchase these dough tubes at almost every supermarket, and the ingredient list is longer than it should be. When you peel back the cardboard, the cylinder pops to reveal a piece of dough in the same shape as its packaging. Unwind the dough and there are eight perfect triangles. You roll each of these up again up to create an instant crescent roll.

My second year in Switzerland, and for the first time ever, I made my own homemade crescent rolls (Nussgipfel) with a yeasted dough and a hazelnut filling. I couldn't believe how easy they were to make and how well they turned out. Why hadn't I tried this before? It was a turning point for me and a gateway to more complex Swiss recipes.

A Nussgipfel is an absolute classic Swiss bakery item. You can find these crescent rolls with a ground hazelnut or almond filling (Mandelgipfel) at almost every bakery in Switzerland. Bakers use either puff pastry or a yeasted dough. Sometimes leftover biscuits are added to the ground nut filling.

Switzerland has a number of nut-filled pastries similar to the Nussgipfel. An Appenzell version has a straight form. Yet another hazelnut-filled pastry with a yeasted dough, the Meitschibei ('girl's legs'), has a finer, U-shaped form. In French-speaking Switzerland, the Meitschibei is sometimes referred to as a Croissant viennois.

When you bake a batch of Nussgipfel at home, I hope you'll feel the same satisfaction I did when I made them for the first time. You can do this! It's so worth it.

5 PETITS PAINS À LA CONFITURE

Preparation Time
approx. 2 hours 30 minutes
bake for 20-25 minutes

Quantity
Makes 9 rolls.

INGREDIENTS

Dough:

- 300 g (2 to 2 ½ cups) all-purpose or bread flour
- 1 tablespoon sugar
- ½ teaspoon salt
- 40 g (3 tablespoons) unsalted butter, softened
- 1 egg, lightly beaten
- 10 g (⅓ oz) fresh yeast, crumbled (or 3 ½ g / 1 ⅛ teaspoons dry yeast)
- 150 ml (⅔ cup) milk, lukewarm

Confiture:

- Use your favorite jam (make sure it has a very thick consistency) or make your own (see p. 46).

Brush on top:

- 1 egg, beaten

INSTRUCTIONS

1. In a large bowl, whisk together 300 g (or start with 2 cups) of flour, the sugar and the salt. Add the softened butter in pieces, but do not mix it in. Make a well in the center of the mixture. Add the lightly beaten egg. Set aside.

2. Separately, add the yeast to the lukewarm milk. Let it sit for a few minutes and then stir until the yeast has fully dissolved. Pour into the center of the flour mixture with the egg in the large bowl. Stir together until a dough forms.

3. Knead the dough by hand on a lightly floured surface, or use an electric mixer with a dough hook, for approximately 10 minutes. Add additional flour as needed, one tablespoon at a time, if the dough is too wet and sticky. When the dough has become smooth and elastic, place it in a bowl covered with a damp kitchen towel. Let it rise for about 1-2 hours or until it has doubled in size.

4. After the dough has risen, divide it into nine equal pieces. Roll out the dough to about 3 mm thick (about 1/10 of an inch) into an elongated oval. Spread a thin layer of jam in the middle of the dough, staying about 1-2 cm (about ½ inch) away from the edge (see diagram, p. 45).

   Please note: If the jam is a bit runny or is spread too thickly across the dough, it increases the chances of it spilling out of the rolls when they're baked. A little bit is OK, but you don't want to lose it all!

5. Now roll up the dough. First, start by folding over about 1-2 cm (about ½ an inch) of dough, then continue to roll and fold over the dough. Keep gently pinching the ends as you roll up the dough to keep them together. When you finish creating the roll, make sure the seam is on the bottom. Gently flatten the roll, and then continue this process with the eight remaining pieces. Then, let them rest for about 30 minutes on a baking sheet lined with parchment paper.

6. Pinch the ends of the rolls again to seal them and press down gently to flatten them slightly. Brush the rolls with the beaten egg. Then, take a pair of kitchen shears, and make a deep lengthwise cut—almost completely to the bottom of the dough layers, but not quite—in the middle of the top of the roll. You should start with the two ends of the kitchen shears about 2-3 cm (¾ to 1 inch) away from the edge of the dough. The rolls should then open up to reveal the jam inside.

7. Bake the rolls for about 20-25 minutes at 180°C / 350°F until they become golden brown. Place on a wire rack to cool.

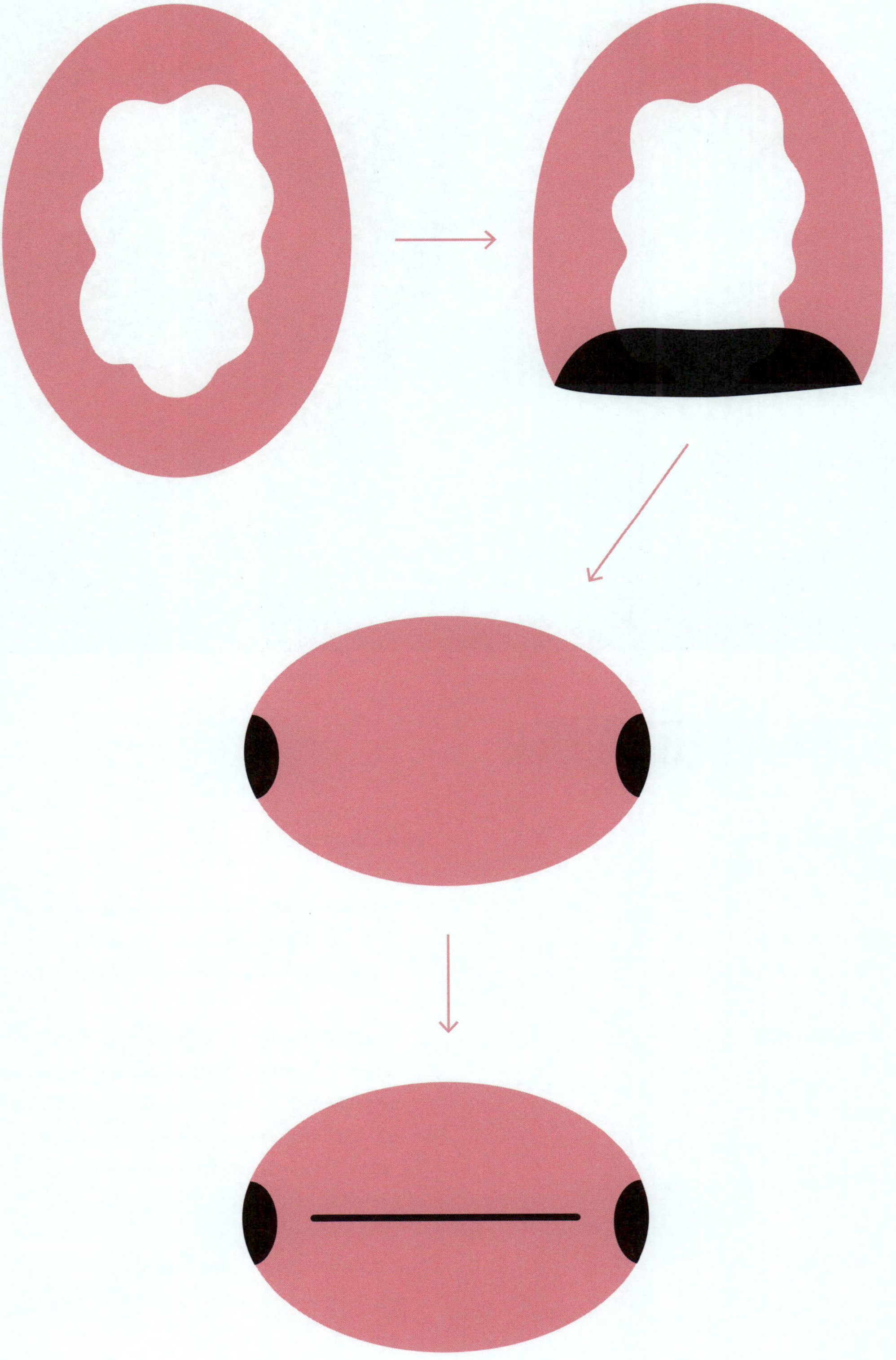

STRAWBERRY JAM

Preparation Time
approx. 45 minutes

Quantity
Makes about 150 ml (2/3 cup).

INGREDIENTS

- 250 g (approx. 2 cups) fresh or frozen whole strawberries
- 100 g (½ cup) sugar
- 2 tablespoons lemon juice

INSTRUCTIONS

1. Puree the fresh, whole, stemmed strawberries (or frozen strawberries that have completely thawed) with an upright or immersion blender.

2. Add the pureed strawberries to a medium saucepan and stir them together with the sugar and lemon juice. Bring the mixture to a boil, and then simmer for about 30 minutes over low to medium heat, stirring frequently, until it thickens.

3. Let the jam cool to room temperature, and then place it in the refrigerator to chill completely.

A JAMMY ROLL WITH A PROVOCATIVE SHAPE

When I opened the oven door, my friend giggled a bit when she saw the shape of the rolls I was making. Cut down the middle, the rolls open as they bake to reveal multiple layers of pastry and bright red jam. Perhaps you can imagine them representing a crude imitation of the female anatomy. You certainly would not be the first person to do so!

With this distinct shape and a jam filling, it becomes a Petit pain à la confiture in French-speaking Switzerland. When filled with a vanilla cream (Petit pain à la vanille), these little sweet breads often carry the name of Vanillerollen on the German-speaking side of the country. Bakers will sometimes brush a sweet glaze on top of the rolls after they come out of the oven.

I had seen the vanilla cream versions of these pastries before, having tried one for the first time from a bakery in La Chaux-de-Fonds (Neuchâtel). Years later, on vacation with my family in Charmey (Fribourg), I came across them again in the same shape, but with a jam filling. Checking in with a friend who grew up in the district of Gruyère, I discovered that she referred to them as Petits pains à la confiture. When I started asking my friends in the city of Neuchâtel about these pastries, I learned I could easily find them at a bakery downtown, a few blocks from where I lived!

The vanilla cream version of these pastries exist in many regions of the country. From my experience, however, the jam-filled version seems more common in French-speaking Switzerland. Also, I find that they exist primarily in the professional sphere, with fewer recipes circulating for home bakers. One benefit of making them yourself is that you're guaranteed the opportunity to enjoy them when still warm from the oven.

Whether you bake them at home or buy them at a Swiss bakery, please try to refrain from making jokes while you eat them!

6 SCHOGGIWEGGLI

Preparation Time

approx. 3 hours 30 minutes
bake for 20-25 minutes

Quantity

Makes 10 buns.

INGREDIENTS

- 500 g (3 ½ to 4 cups) all-purpose or bread flour
- 6 g (1 teaspoon) salt
- 75 g (⅓ cup) unsalted butter, softened
- 20 g fresh yeast, crumbled (or 7 g / 2 ¼ teaspoons dry yeast)
- 300 ml (1 ¼ cups) milk, lukewarm
- 100 g (3 ½ oz) dark chocolate, chopped

Brush on before baking:

- 1 egg, beaten

INSTRUCTIONS

1. Whisk 500 g (or start with 3 ½ cups) of flour and the salt together in a large bowl. Add the softened butter in pieces, but do not mix it in. Make a well in the center. Set aside.

2. Add the yeast to the lukewarm milk. Let it sit for a few minutes and then stir together until the yeast has dissolved.

3. Pour the yeast mixture into the middle of the flour mixture. Stir until a soft dough forms.

4. Knead the dough for approximately 10 minutes by hand on a lightly floured surface or use an electric mixer with a dough hook. Add additional flour as needed, one tablespoon at a time, if the dough is too wet and sticky. When the dough has become smooth and elastic, add the chopped dark chocolate to the bowl and knead it into the dough by hand until well combined. Then, place the dough in a bowl covered with a damp kitchen towel. Let the dough rise for about 1-2 hours, or until doubled in size.

5. After the dough has finished its first rise, divide it into ten equal parts. Moving your hand in a circular motion over and around the individual pieces of dough, form them into oval shapes. Try to keep the chocolate pieces hidden in the dough and not exposed on the surface. Flatten each of the rolls slightly with your hand.

6. Place the buns evenly spaced on a baking sheet lined with parchment paper. Cover them loosely with a clean kitchen towel and let them rise for about 30 minutes.

7. Brush the buns with the beaten egg. Then, using a pair of kitchen shears, make a series of about 3-4 cuts, lengthwise across the surface of the bun to create a row of triangular points.

8. Bake for about 20-25 minutes at 200°C / 400°F until they become golden brown. Remove and place on a wire rack to cool.

ENTICING LITTLE CHOCOLATE BUNS FROM BASEL

You can find small buns filled with chocolate chunks at bakeries throughout Switzerland, but these sweet treats have a strong connection with Basel. Developed in 1975 by Anton Bachmann of Confiserie Bachmann, the oval-shaped Schoggiweggli have distinct cuts across the top. Today, many bakeries and supermarkets around the city make their own versions of these buns. I like them for breakfast or an afternoon snack.

Since Confiserie Bachmann started making this local specialty, they have always cut the chocolate into pieces by hand. I have read that people who want a lot of chocolate in their Schoggiweggli should look for flatter buns at the bakery. A higher proportion of heavy chocolate pieces can prevent the dough from rising, giving less height to the bun.

The name Schoggiweggli combines two Swiss German words: *schoggi* for 'chocolate', and *weggli* for a 'bread roll.' A Weggli, or Petit pain au lait in French-speaking Switzerland, however, has a crease in its middle. These little breads, just like the Schoggiweggli, are especially popular with children. At the same time, people of all ages love these chocolate buns. They are a wonderfully sweet tradition from Basel.

You will notice that my recipe does not contain any added sugar. These rolls rely on the chunks of dark chocolate for their sweetness. I did this in homage to the popular Swiss snack for children that involves simply making a sandwich out of a soft bread roll and a chocolate bar. If you would like to sweeten up the dough as well, feel free to add a few tablespoons of sugar to this recipe.

7 SALÉE ORMONANCHE

Preparation Time
approx. 3 hours
bake for 25-30 minutes

Quantity
Makes one yeasted cake with 8-10 servings.

INGREDIENTS

Dough:

- 250 g (1 ¾ to 2 cups) all-purpose or bread flour
- ½ teaspoon salt
- 60 g (4 tablespoons) unsalted butter, softened
- 10 g (about ⅓ oz) fresh yeast, crumbled (or 3 ½ g / 1 ⅛ teaspoons dry yeast)
- 150 ml (⅔ cups) milk, lukewarm

Filling:

- 200 g (¾ cup + 3 tablespoons) cassonade sugar*
- 100 g (¾ cup) all-purpose flour
- 2 teaspoons cinnamon
- 100 ml (scant ½ cup) heavy cream (35% milk fat)
- 100 ml (⅔ cup) dry white wine (e.g., Chasselas)
- 85 g (6 tablespoons) unsalted butter

*You can substitute this ingredient with turbinado sugar.

INSTRUCTIONS

1. In a large bowl, whisk together 250 g (or start with 1 ¾ cups) of flour and the salt. Add the softened butter to the bowl in pieces, but do not mix it in. Make a well in the center. Set aside.

2. In a small bowl, add the yeast to the lukewarm milk. Let it sit for a few minutes, and then whisk together until the yeast has completely dissolved.

3. Pour the yeast mixture into the center of the flour mixture in the large bowl. Stir together until a soft dough forms.

4. On a lightly floured surface, knead the dough for about 10 minutes, or use an electric mixture with a dough hook, until it becomes smooth and elastic. Add additional flour as needed, one tablespoon at a time, if the dough is too wet and sticky.

5. Place the dough in a large bowl and cover it with a damp kitchen towel. Let the dough rise for about 1-2 hours or until it doubles in size.

6. Line a round pan with a diameter of about 28 cm (11 inches) with parchment paper. Gently roll out the dough into a large circle. Press dough into the pan. Make sure the sides of the

dough are about 1-2 cm (½ to ¾ of an inch) high. Cover the dough again with the damp kitchen towel and let it rest for 30 minutes.

7. Sift together the first three ingredients for the filling: cassonade sugar, flour and cinnamon. Use a fork to prick the dough in the bottom of the pan (not the sides). Then spread it into the pan with the prepared dough.

8. Separately, stir the wine and cream together. Pour this mixture evenly over the sugar, flour and cinnamon in the pan. Then, cut the cold butter into wide, thin pieces and place them evenly over the top of all the filling ingredients already in the pan.

9. Bake for about 25-30 minutes in an oven preheated to 200°C / 400°F. Take the cake out when the outer crust has browned and the filling has set. Let it sit in the pan for about 10 minutes, and then place the cake on a wire rack to cool.

A 'SALTY' TART IS A MISNOMER FROM VAUD

The Salée ormonanche belongs to a family of 'salty' cakes made in the canton of Vaud—although this name belies their sweet ingredients. These yeasted cakes, made with an enriched bread dough base, all have toppings that contain sugar. The use of *sallaye* or *salée* to describe a style of cake dates back to the 17th century in Switzerland. Over the years, people have continued to use this name for these special tart-like cakes which often have a yeasted bread base. At the same time, I have also seen the Salée ormonanche made with a short crust pastry *(pate brisée).*

The most well-known of these Vaudois cakes, in my opinion, is the Salée au sucre, which has a sweet cream topping. Both professional bakers and home cooks make this popular cake. Another cake of this type, the Salée de la Vallée d'Illiez, has a slightly crunchy *sablé* topping. As its name suggests, it comes from Illiez Valley in the canton of Valais, close to the border with Vaud. You make it with flour, sugar, butter and cinnamon. A friend of mine first tried this cake at the Cabane d'Anthème, and he always raves about it.

What I like best about the Salée ormonanche is that it incorporates characteristics of these two cakes—the creamy topping of the Salée au sucre with the sandy texture of the Salée de la Vallée d'Illiez. The name for the Salée ormonanche comes from its region of origin, the Ormont Valley. Residents of the mountain villages of Ormont-Dessous (below) and Ormont-Dessus (above) are known as *Les Ormonans.*

Another distinct difference for the Ormonanche cake is the type of sugar used. Instead of white sugar, you add cassonade sugar to the topping mixture. This naturally brown cane sugar has a granulated texture and is not soft like an American brown sugar.

I think this cake, with a rustic appearance, tastes best the same day you bake it. It would be ideal for a Sunday brunch with people seated all around the table to enjoy it. Or serve it for dessert with a cold glass of Bitter des Diablerets on ice, an herbal aperitif from this same region.

8 MERISHAUSER BIENENSTICH

Preparation Time

approx. 3 hours

bake for 25-35 minutes

Quantity

Makes one cake.

8-10 servings

INGREDIENTS

Sponge:

- 300 g (2 to 2 ½ cups) all-purpose or bread flour
- 50 g (¼ cup) sugar, divided
- 10 g (about ⅓ oz) fresh yeast, crumbled (3 ½ g / 1 ⅛ teaspoons dry yeast)
- 225 g (1 cup) milk, lukewarm

Remaining dough ingredients:

- 40 g (3 tablespoons) unsalted butter, softened
- 1 egg
- ¼ teaspoon salt

Hazelnut-honey lid:

- 50 g (3 ½ tablespoons) unsalted butter, softened
- 50 g (3 tablespoons + 1 teaspoon) honey
- 25 g (2 tablespoons) sugar
- a pinch of salt
- 80 g (½ cup + 1 tablespoon) whole hazelnuts, chopped into small pieces

Vanilla cream filling:

- 225 g (2 cups) powdered sugar
- 115 g (½ cup) unsalted butter, softened
- 1 teaspoon vanilla extract or paste
- 2-3 tablespoons milk

INSTRUCTIONS

Dough

1. Make the dough. In a large bowl, whisk together 300 g (or start with 2 cups) of flour and 25 grams (2 tablespoons) of the sugar. Make a well in the center and set aside.

2. Separately, add the yeast and the remaining 25 grams (2 tablespoons) of sugar to the lukewarm milk. Let it sit for a few minutes and then whisk it together until it's well combined.

3. Pour the yeast mixture into the center of the large bowl with the flour mixture, creating a puddle of liquid surrounded by flour. Gently stir the yeast mixture, pulling in a little (not all) of the flour from the sides of the puddle to create a paste. Cover the bowl with a damp kitchen towel and let it rest for about 30 minutes.

4. Remove the towel from the bowl. The mixture should have become a bit bubbly and foamy. Add the softened butter in pieces, the egg and the salt. Using an electric mixer with a paddle attachment, mix the yeasted batter for about

8-10 minutes on the lowest setting (or stir it vigorously by hand), until it becomes smooth and pulls away from the sides of the bowl when stirred. Add additional flour as needed, one tablespoon at a time, if the dough seems too wet and sticky. Leave the batter in the bowl, cover with the damp kitchen towel again and let it rise for about 1-2 hours, until the batter has nearly doubled in size.

5. Line a springform pan with a diameter of about 23 cm (9 inches) with parchment paper. Pour in the cake batter and cover with the damp kitchen towel. Let it rise for another hour.

Hazelnut-honey lid

6. Prepare the topping for the cake. Mix together the butter, sugar and honey. Stir in the chopped hazelnuts. Poke several deep holes with a skewer or toothpick into the top of the cake. Then, add small spoonfuls of the mixture onto the surface of the soft dough and carefully spread them to form an even layer.

7. Bake in the lower part of the oven for 25-35 minutes at 180°C / 350°F until the surface of the cake becomes a light golden brown. Let it cool in the pan for about 10 minutes, and then use a sharp knife to carefully loosen any of the topping that has stuck to the sides of the pan. Gently transfer the cake to a wire rack to cool.

Vanilla cream filling

8. When the cake has completely cooled, prepare the vanilla cream filling. Sift the powdered sugar into a large bowl. Then, add the butter, vanilla and one tablespoon of milk at a time, beating everything together by hand or with an electric mixer until it creates a smooth, spreadable filling.

9. Use a serrated bread knife to carefully slice the cake horizontally, creating two even layers. Spread the frosting evenly on the bottom layer and then gently put on the top layer of the cake.

Please note: If you plan to make the cake ahead of time, hold off on cutting it and adding the frosting layer until just before serving it.

SCHAFFHAUSEN'S HAZELNUT VARIANT OF THE BEESTING CAKE

With its sweet nutty topping and soft spongy cake, the Merishauser Bienenstich reminds me of an American coffee cake. Unlike these cakes, however, this Swiss version contains yeast instead of baking powder. It comes from Merishausen (Schaffhausen) and has a sweet vanilla cream filling and a crunchy hazelnut lid. I think it works particularly well for breakfast, second breakfast or brunch.

Bienenstich cakes exist elsewhere in German-speaking Switzerland, as well as in Germany. These cakes have flaked almonds on their surface, instead of the chopped hazelnut topping used in Merishausen. This cake was the creation of the Leu family bakery, which opened in the late 19th century. With the closure of the bakery in 1991, and the real prospect of this cake disappearing for good, Ruth Hoyer at the Tanner & Hoyer farm shop in Merishausen revived this culinary tradition. You can find the Merishauser Bienenstich at her farm shop, which she provides to loyal clients as well as restaurants.

The word *bienenstich* means 'beesting' in German. One popular legend suggests the cake earned this name because of an incident that occurred during the 15th century. Apparently two bakers from Andernach, Germany, threw a swarm of bees at people from a neighboring town that were attacking their village. To celebrate, they created the Bienenstich cake to commemorate the victory.

When I make this cake at home, I use a 'sponge' technique, in which you prepare a pre-dough paste in the center of a flour mixture. This method adds a certain lightness to the texture of the cake. Honestly, I absolutely love this honey-sweetened bready cake, and I consider it one of my favorite Swiss food discoveries.

9 ANDEERER QUARKINI

from Torsten Rönisch, Hotel Restaurant Capricorns in Wergenstein (Graubünden)

Preparation Time

approx. 1 hour 30 minutes
fry in oil for 7-10 minutes

Quantity

Makes approx. 25-30 Quarkini.

INGREDIENTS

Dough

- 250 g (2 cups) all-purpose flour
- 250 g (1 cup + 1 ½ tablespoons) quark*
- 125 g (⅔ cup) sugar
- 2 eggs
- 2 teaspoons baking powder
- 1 teaspoon vanilla paste or extract

Cinnamon sugar

- 4 tablespoons sugar
- 1 tablespoon cinnamon

*You can use sour cream or plain yogurt as a substitute for quark.

INSTRUCTIONS

1. Mix the flour with all the remaining ingredients together to form a thick batter.

2. Place the dough in the refrigerator for at least one hour or up to 24 hours. While the dough rests in the fridge, whisk the cinnamon and sugar together and set aside.

3. Heat vegetable oil for frying in a Dutch oven or in a deep fat fryer until it reaches 170°C / 340°F.

4. Use an ice cream scoop or two spoons to make spheres of dough with a diameter of nearly 4 cm (1 ½ inches) and gently place them into the hot oil. Let them fry in the oil for approximately 7-10 minutes until they become golden brown on all sides.

5. Remove the quarkini from the oil. Place them directly on a baking sheet lined with paper towels to soak up the excess oil.

6. Add the cinnamon sugar to a bowl and roll the warm quarkini in this mixture until they are evenly coated. You can place them on a wire rack to cool, but they are best served warm.

SWISS BEIGNETS FROM A MOUNTAIN RESTAURANT

Situated at an elevation of about 1,500 meters above sea level (over 4,900 feet), the Hotel Restaurant Capricorns in the Beverin Nature Park commands a stunning view of the Val Schons (Scams Valley). Located in Wergenstein, with fewer than 100 residents, the Capricorns is the only restaurant in the village. Head Chef Torsten Rönisch focuses on ingredients and traditional dishes from the region. His recipe for Quarkini (also known as Quarkbällchen), a dessert featured on the summer menu during my visit, highlights this ultra-local approach.

Built in the 1930s, the hotel was once the holiday home of the Metall- und Uhrenarbeiterverband ('metal and watch workers' association'). No longer used for this purpose, a special foundation was created in 2005 to establish the Center da Capricorns. This center incorporates the hotel restaurant, the headquarters and exhibition space for the Beverin Nature Park and a satellite campus for the ZHAW Forschungsgruppe Tourismus und nachhaltige Entwicklung (Research Unit for Tourism and Sustainable Development of the Zurich University of Applied Sciences). This award-winning public-private partnership continues to benefit both locals and visitors to this mountain village.

Guests of the hotel have front-door access to the beauty of its natural surroundings and outdoor activities hosted by the nature park. At the end of your day, the cozy, comfortable wood-paneled dining room of the hotel awaits you, with a modern interpretation of classic Bündner dishes. The French restaurant reviewer, Gault-Millau, has written about this restaurant in its Swiss guidebook—yet another reason that it definitely warrants a visit. Switzerland has this never-ending capacity to surprise me with these exceptional restaurants in remote locations with absolutely breathtaking views.

Chef Rönisch, who has experience working in five-star hotels in Dresden and Berlin, now finds inspiration in reinterpreting Swiss regional dishes. He arrived at the Capricorns in 2011. His cozy kitchen has a relaxed, friendly atmosphere. He told me he appreciates having the creative freedom afforded him in this environment.

On my last night at the hotel, I ordered the Andeerer Quarkbällchen for dessert. Chef Rönisch served these beignets, flavored with tonka beans, alongside fresh strawberries and an organic elderflower sorbet. When you visit, you will notice that his delicious handmade ice cream features heavily in the dessert menu.

If you're not familiar with quark, as was the case when I first moved to Switzerland, this creamy fresh cheese product has not been pressed, so it has a spreadable texture. Known as *séré* in French, this milk product has a high protein content. I have seen it described as something between yogurt and cottage cheese. (I also use this ingredient to make puff pastry for Apricot Jalousien, p. 65). When using quark in a pastry dough or cake batter, I find it helps create a lighter and moister texture.

The Capricorns restaurant sources the quark for these beignets from the *sennerei* (creamery) in the village of Andeer down in the valley. Run by cheesemaker Maria Meyer and her husband Martin Bienerth, this creamery is known for using organic milk from a handful of local farms. The milk comes from cows that still have their horns, as Maria and Martin disagree with the practice of dehorning. When you visit the hotel, I highly recommend a visit to this small creamery in the village as well (the mineral baths in town are also quite nice).

When I make quarkini at home with Chef Rönisch's recipe, I form the dough into a slightly bigger sphere than the ones he served us at the Capricorns restaurant. My quarkini are meant to be eaten with your hands, like those you find at bakeries in German-speaking Switzerland. In the United States, I would refer to these as generously portioned 'doughnut holes'. You can also make them smaller, like those you would find at the restaurant. I really recommend going to Wergenstein and tasting them yourself! After a long hike in the mountains surrounding the hotel, it's a wonderful way to end the day with this sweet, fried treat.

HOTEL RESTAURANT CAPRICORNS

Veia Cantunala 51
7433 Wergenstein
+41 (0)81 630 71 72
hotel@capricorns.ch
capricorns.ch

10 APRICOT JALOUSIEN

Preparation Time

approx. 2 hours 30 minutes

bake for approx. 20 minutes

Quantity

Makes approx. 15 pastries.

INGREDIENTS

Pastry dough

- 250 g (2 cups) all-purpose flour
- ½ teaspoon salt
- 125 g (½ cup + 1 tablespoon) unsalted butter, cold
- 200 g (¾ cup + 2 tablespoons) quark*

Fruit topping

- apricots, pitted and thinly sliced
- one egg, beaten

Additional toppings (after baking):

- honey
- chopped nuts such as pistachios
- powdered sugar

*You can use *crème fraîche* as a substitute for quark.

INSTRUCTIONS

1. Make the dough. Whisk the flour and salt together in a bowl. Add the cold butter in pieces to the bowl and cut them into the flour mixture using a pastry blender or two knives. Stir in the quark until well combined, but do not knead the dough. Wrap the dough in parchment paper and place in the refrigerator for about 30 minutes.

2. On a lightly floured surface, roll out the dough into a rectangle about 3 mm (1/10 of an inch) thick. Fold over one-third of the short side of the rectangle toward the middle. Then, fold over one-third of the other short side of the rectangle toward the middle, creating three layers of dough (see diagram). Cover and refrigerate for about 30 minutes. Repeat the process, rolling out the dough and folding it in the other direction. Cover and refrigerate again for another 30 minutes.

3. Preheat the oven to 200°C / 400°F.

4. Roll out the dough one last time to about 3 mm (1/10 of an inch) thick. Cut the puff pastry into approximately 15 rectangles about 7 x 9 cm (2 ¾ x 3 ½ inches). Lay them out on a baking sheet lined with parchment paper.

5. Place a cascading row of apricot slices in the center of the puff pastry rectangles. Brush the edges of the puff pastry with some of the beaten egg.

6. Bake for about 20 minutes, until the puff pastry has risen and turned golden brown. While they are still warm, use a pastry brush to spread a thin layer of warmed honey on the apricots.

7. Give them a dusting of powdered sugar and then sprinkle on some of the nuts.

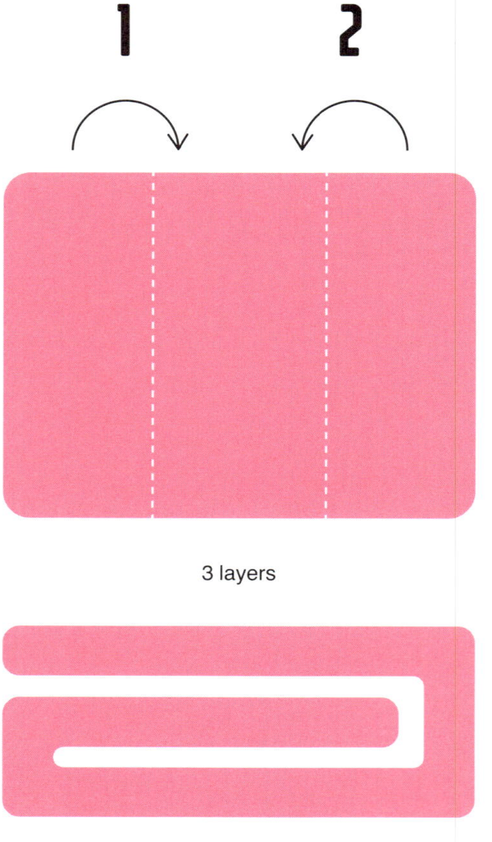

PUFF PASTRY 'BLINDS' WITH APRICOTS

At Swiss bakeries, especially during the stone fruit season, you may find a pastry known as a Jalousie. After seeing these for years, I always assumed the name was French, as the word *jalousie* means 'jealousy.' I imagined people would feel jealous watching you eat one of these pastries, so that became my unfounded rationale for the name. It turned out to be completely wrong.

The answer finally came to me during a visit to the Crest bakery in Flims (Graubünden). When I asked the person behind the counter about the etymology of the Jalousie, she kindly explained that *jalousie* (*jalousien*, plural) means Venetian blinds in German. The pastry earned this name because the sliced fruit is layered in a cascading way like the blinds made for windows. Later, when I looked up *jalousie* in a French-English dictionary, I learned that this word, in addition to 'jealousy,' also means Venetian blinds in French. So, while many bakery items in Switzerland have different names in French and German (e.g., Zopf vs. Tresse or Mailänderli vs. Milanais), the Jalousie pastry is generally known in both linguistic regions by the same name. In Italian-speaking Switzerland, however, this pastry is not called by this term. Instead, you might see it described simply as, Sfogliatine alle albicocche ('puff pastry with apricots').

For my first attempts at these pastry blinds, I must admit that I used premade, store-bought puff pastry. I thought preparing these butter layers myself would just be too time-consuming and not worth the effort. I came to realize, however, that industrial puff pastry often contains margarine-like products, instead of real butter. So, I now make my own, using a short-cut puff pastry method that calls for quark. I won't buy store-bought puff pastry again—unless I'm in a hurry and it contains 100% butter.

When you make these pastries with apricots from Valais, you'll have a uniquely Swiss dessert. Did you know that there are over 70 different varieties of apricots found in this Swiss canton? For decades, the Luizet was just about the only variety of apricot in Switzerland. Since the 1990s, dozens of other varieties have been introduced in Valais. Why? To have a selection of different apricots more durable for transport across the country. These new varieties also helped create a longer season, as they included early- and late-season apricots.

Valais apricots grow primarily in the Rhone Valley, on the south side of the river between Sierre and Vernayaz. This area has a microclimate with sunny, dry conditions where apricots can thrive. According to Patrimoine Culinaire Suisse, the first known documentation of apricots in Valais comes from a book by Dr. Schiner, *Description du département du Simplon*, published in 1812.

Still warm from the oven, Apricot Jalousien taste good on their own or with a scoop of vanilla ice cream. Make sure to share your pastries though, so people don't have to feel jealous of your sweet 'blinds'!

11 RISSOLES AUX POIRES

Preparation Time

approx. 2 hours 30 minutes
bake for 15-17 mins

Quantity

Makes 10-12 rissoles.

INGREDIENTS

Filling:

- 500 g (1 lb) pears,* peeled, halved and cored
- about 300-350 ml (1 ¼ to 1 ½ cups) water
- 50 g (½ cup + 1 tablespoon) raisins
- juice of one organic lemon
- 2 tablespoons dry red wine
- 1 cinnamon stick (or ¼ teaspoon ground cinnamon)
- 1 whole star anise
- 50-65 g (¼ - ⅓ cups) sugar

Dough:

- 250 g (2 cups) all-purpose flour
- 1 tablespoon sugar
- ½ teaspoon salt
- 125 g (9 tablespoons) unsalted butter, cold
- 2-3 tablespoons cold water
- 1-2 tablespoons vodka (or more cold water)

To seal the edges of the dough:

- 1 egg white

To brush on before baking:

- 1 egg yolk whisked with 1 teaspoon of milk

*Choose a pear variety that is very firm and typically used for cooking or baking. In Switzerland, and particularly in the canton of Geneva, look for the Charlon, Blesson or Marlioz varieties.

INSTRUCTIONS

1. Make the filling. Add all the ingredients, except the sugar, to a medium saucepan. Bring the mixture to a boil, and then simmer for about 30-60 minutes.

2. When the pears and raisins have softened, remove the cinnamon stick and star anise and mash the mixture with a potato masher to break up the pears into smaller pieces. After that, take half of the mixture and blend it into a puree with either an immersion or upright blender. Return all the mixture to the medium saucepan, mix 50-65 g of sugar and bring it to a boil. Once it's boiling, reduce the heat and let it simmer until it thickens, stirring frequently. Remove the pan from the heat and let it cool to room temperature. Then refrigerate the filling and start preparing the dough.

3. Make the dough. Whisk the flour, sugar and salt together in a large bowl. Next, add the cold butter, in pieces, to the bowl. Using a food processor, pastry blender or two knives, cut the

butter into the flour mixture, until it becomes the size of small pebbles. Make a well in the center of the bowl and add two tablespoons of cold water and one tablespoon of vodka. Stir together just until a dough forms, adding additional tablespoon(s) of water and vodka as needed. Refrigerate the dough for 30-60 minutes.

4. When the dough and filling mixture have chilled, roll out the dough on a lightly floured surface to about 2-3 mm thick (about 1⁄10 of an inch). Cut circles into the dough that have a diameter of about 10 cm (4 inches). I invert a small bowl onto the dough and use a sharp knife to cut around it.

5. Start by placing one circle of dough directly on to a baking sheet lined with parchment paper. Use your fingers to wet the edges of the dough circle with some egg white. Then, add about a tablespoon of filling to the center of the circle. Next, let the middle of the dough circle rest on your workspace, and fold the circle in half, pressing the edges together to form a half-circle rissole. Lay the rissole on its side on the baking sheet and press down the edges with a fork to further seal the edges of the dough. Repeat this process with the remaining dough circles.

6. Brush the surface of the rissoles with the beaten egg mixed with milk. Then, bake them for about 15-17 minutes at 200°C / 400°F until their surface becomes a light golden brown. Place them on a wire rack to cool.

GENEVA'S COOKED PEAR HAND PIES

Rissoles aux poires have a history both in the Savoy region of France and in the canton of Geneva. The term *rissole* (patois: *rzulè*) may have its origins in the Latin word *russeolus*, which means 'reddish'. Perhaps the connection also lies with the French word, *rissoler*, which means 'to brown.' These references to color could be attributed to the filling, which can take on a brownish-red-like hue, especially when bakers add a bit of red wine to the boiled pears.

Traditionally made during the Christmas holiday season, Rissoles aux poires can have either a short crust or puff pastry wrapper. Short crust pastry seems the most common for these hand pies, particularly for homemade versions. They contain a cooked pear filling sometimes with the addition of raisins, dried currants or quince. This thick pear compote is often seasoned with cinnamon and can include a variety of other ingredients, such as lemon zest, candied orange peel, kirsch and more.

In Geneva, certain varieties of pears are favored for these pastries. These can include the Charlon, Blesson or Marlioz. At farms like Ferme Courtois in Versoix, you can buy Poires à rissoles, another moniker for the Marlioz variety, specifically named for these regional pastries. Geneva has about 80 hectares devoted to fruit production, mostly apples, with pears in second place. The Marlioz represents an old variety of pear recognized as part of Geneva's culinary heritage. These pears have a firm texture that works well for cooking and baking.

Considering you must cook and cool the filling in advance, these pear pastries do take time to prepare. And then, the people you love will likely eat them all in about one-fifth of the time it takes you to make them! They will be grateful for your hard work though, and the holidays are the perfect time of year for baking projects just like these.

12 PANE DEI MORTI

Preparation Time

approx. 15-20 minutes
bake for about 15-20 minutes

Quantity

Makes 10 little breads.

INGREDIENTS

- 100 g (⅔ cup) ground almonds
- 1 egg white
- 75 g (5 tablespoons) sweetened chestnut puree
- 84 g (¼ cup) honey
- 25 g (2 tablespoons) candied orange peel, finely chopped
- 2 tablespoons amaretto
- zest of one organic lemon
- 150 g (1 cup + 3 tablespoons) all-purpose flour
- 2 tablespoons cocoa powder
- 1 teaspoon cinnamon
- ½ teaspoon baking soda
- ¼ teaspoon nutmeg
- ¼ teaspoon salt

Sprinkle on after baking:

- powdered sugar

INSTRUCTIONS

1. Toast the ground almonds in a frying pan over medium-high heat for about 3-5 minutes, stirring frequently to avoid burning them, until they become fragrant. When they're ready, remove them from the heat and set them aside to cool down.

2. In a large bowl, whisk the egg white until it becomes foamy. Then, stir together the next seven ingredients until well combined: toasted ground almonds (cooled), chestnut puree, honey, candied orange peel, amaretto and lemon zest.

3. Whisk together the following dry ingredients in a separate bowl: flour, cocoa powder, cinnamon, baking soda, nutmeg and salt. Then, sift this mixture into the large bowl with the wet ingredients. Stir everything together just until dough forms. Do not overmix.

4. On a lightly floured surface, form the dough into ten elongated ovals, pinching the ends to create points on both sides of the dough. They should be about 11 ½ cm (4 ½ inches) in length and about 2 cm (¾ inch) thick. With a sharp serrated knife, make a cut lengthwise across the dough. Place them on a baking sheet lined with parchment paper and bake for about 15-20 minutes at 200°C / 400°F.

5. Take them out of the oven and cool on the baking sheet for about 10 minutes. Then cool on a wire rack. Dust with powdered sugar before serving.

TICINO'S BREAD OF THE DEAD

My family and I were visiting Lugano in the fall, when I happened upon a little bakery. The bakery had just pulled out a pan of elongated little breads. I watched as the baker coated them generously with powdered sugar. A handwritten paper sign placed on one of the baking sheets read, "Pane dei morti, Fr. 2.50."

Afterwards, as we walked in the park along Lago di Lugano (Lake Lugano), I ate the little 'bread of the dead' as my afternoon snack. The bread had a human-like form. It tasted of chocolate and bitter almonds, and I wished I had bought more!

The period around All Saints' Day on the first of November and the Day of the Dead (All Souls' Day) on the second of November is prime time for Pane dei morti both in Ticino and in neighboring Italy. These little breads can contain a mixture of dried fruit, chestnuts, pine nuts, leftover biscuits, spices and more.

Pane dei morti should not be confused with the Ossi di morto ('bones of the dead'). You'll also find these crisp almond or hazelnut biscuits in Ticino around this same time of year. Research by Patrimoine Culinaire Suisse suggests that these sweet breads evolved from the ancient practice of distributing bread to the mourners after a funeral.

There are so many variations in recipes for the Pane dei morti, which are actually more like large biscuits, especially those with a crisper texture. I add cocoa powder and a generous splash of amaretto to the dough for these biscuits, to try to recreate the memory of that wonderful afternoon snack from Lugano.

IV

CAKES & TARTS
KUCHEN UND TORTEN
GÂTEAUX ET TARTES

IV. CAKES & TARTS

Swiss cakes and tarts show up at times of celebration and as part of daily life. Some exist almost exclusively in the professional sphere, such as the Carac (p. 123) or Solothurner Torte (p. 133). Others, like a typically Swiss apple tart—generally known as Apfelwähe in Swiss German, Tarte aux pommes in French or Torta di mele in Italian—exist throughout the country, both at home and in bakeries (you'll find a recipe on my blog). Then, there are cakes with a radius of enjoyment that has expanded beyond their place of origin, such as the Tuorta da Nuschs (Bündner Nusstorte), a walnut cake from Graubünden (p. 99) or the Torta di pane, a leftover bread cake from Ticino (p. 83). When asked, most people throughout Switzerland will typically be familiar with these cakes.

I love Switzerland's 'national' cakes and tarts, but I especially love learning about all the regional recipes as well. The Schlorzifladen, with a dried pear filling from Appenzell, is a particular favorite (p. 129). From the canton where I live, Neuchâtel, I really enjoy a slice of Gâteau aux noisettes ('hazelnut tart', p. 119) with a cup of milky hot coffee.

You can use the recipes in this chapter to make cakes and tarts for dinner parties, birthdays or just when you need something sweet for your *zvieri* or *quatre-heures* (4 o'clock snack).

13 LEBKUCHEN

Preparation Time
approx. 15 minutes
bake for 35-40 minutes

Quantity
Makes one cake.
10-12 servings

INGREDIENTS

Pastry dough

- 300 g (1 ½ cups) sugar
- 100 g (¼ cup + 1 tablespoon) *birnendicksaft**
- 100 ml (½ cup) light cream (25 % milk fat)
- 2 tablespoons canola oil
- 500 g (4 cups) all-purpose flour
- 1 tablespoon gingerbread spice**
- ¾ teaspoon baking soda
- ½ teaspoon salt
- 350 ml (1 ½ cups) milk

**birnendicksaft* (*birnel* or *jus de poires concentré*), is a concentrated pear syrup. In the US, you can purchase or make your own boiled apple cider, which you can substitute for this ingredient.

**If you want to make your own gingerbread spice, check out my recipe on p. 80.

INSTRUCTIONS

1. Line a rectangular cake pan (about 23 x 33 cm / 9 x 13 inches) with parchment paper. Set aside.

2. In a large bowl, whisk together the first four ingredients until well combined: sugar, *birnendicksaft*, light cream and canola oil. Set aside.

3. Separately, in another bowl, whisk together the following dry ingredients: flour, gingerbread spice, baking soda and salt.

4. Add half the dry ingredients and half the milk to the large bowl with the wet ingredients, stir just until combined. Then, add the remaining ingredients and stir again just until the dry ingredients have been completely absorbed. Do not overmix.

5. Pour the batter in the prepared pan. Bake for 35-40 minutes at 180˚C / 350˚F. You may need to adjust the time depending on the size of the pan. The cake is ready when a toothpick or metal skewer inserted into its center comes out clean.

GINGERBREAD SPICE

INGREDIENTS

- 6 tablespoons ground cinnamon
- 1 teaspoon ground anise seed
- 1 teaspoon ground coriander
- ½ teaspoon ground star anise
- ½ teaspoon ground cloves
- ½ teaspoon ground white pepper
- ½ teaspoon ground ginger
- ½ teaspoon ground cardamom

INSTRUCTIONS

Whisk all the ingredients together and store in a tightly sealed glass jar.

A SOFT, STICKY GINGERBREAD CAKE

Sometimes you just need cake, and gingerbread shouldn't be just for the Advent season. If you agree with one or both of these statements, then this is a great recipe for you. A super-easy, no-fuss tray bake (sheet cake), it is inspired by the softer, stickier spiced breads of central Switzerland.

Overall, Switzerland has many different types of regional gingerbreads. Known as Lebkuchen in German or Läbchueche in Swiss German dialect, each area of Switzerland seems to have its own special take on this sweet, spiced bread, especially popular at Christmas time. For example, Biscômes in French-speaking Switzerland are often passed out by Saint Nicholas to children on December 6. These rectangular gingerbreads typically have a rather dry texture. The round, flat Biberfladen from Appenzell has a similar style. Unlike a Biberli, bakers often make them without an almond paste filling.

In central Switzerland, especially in Luzern, the addition of an ingredient known as *birnendicksaft* helps create a softer, even stickier cake. *Birnendicksaft* is a thick, sweet syrup made from a filtered pear juice concentrate. Some people like using it as an accompaniment for cheese and boiled potatoes. This product resembles, but is different from, the non-filtered Swiss French versions known as *vin cuit* in Fribourg or *raisinée* in Vaud, which can also contain apple juice (for more details, see the recipe for Tarte à la raisinée, p. 137). The round, domed Luzerner Lebkuchen contains *birnendicksaft* in the batter, and it's also brushed on the warm cake after it comes out of the oven.

In the cantons of Schwyz and Uri, as well as Obwalden and Nidwalden, you will also find these softer gingerbread cakes. For example, I have noticed that Lebkuchen recipes from Uri and Schwyz, in particular, often contain vegetable oil as the fat and baking soda as the rising agent. The ones from Schwyz sometimes call for the addition of *birnendicksaft* and recipes from both cantons may include a tablespoon or two of cocoa powder.

The town of Einsiedeln, within the canton of Schwyz, has a special museum devoted to Swiss gingerbread. The Goldapfel ('golden apple') bakery has been producing gingerbread since 1850. Religious pilgrims visiting the impressive baroque abbey in town, about a 5-minute walk from the Goldapfel company, would stop into the shop to pick up some gingerbread. A round Schafböcke, one of its sweet honey pastries, has the image of a sheep lying down pressed into its surface. It represents the ancient practice of sacrificing the first-born male sheep of the year for Easter celebrations. You can visit the small Goldapfel museum to learn about the history of its gingerbread and take home a Schafböcke or Biberli from its shop, which is renovated to look as it did in 1896.

As you can see, Swiss gingerbread includes professionally made creations, like the ones in Einsiedeln, using hand-carved wooden molds to create artistic motifs, as well as spiced pear syrup cakes from Luzern and central Switzerland, and more. My recipe for Lebkuchen borrows from the slightly softer and moister Swiss gingerbreads, made both in bakeries and by home bakers. You can throw this cake together quickly, and it will feed a crowd—whether for breakfast, a morning coffee break or an afternoon snack. For dessert, try serving it with a dollop of whipped cream. And it doesn't have to just be for Christmas!

14 TORTA DI PANE

From Arturo Sartore, Grotto dei Due Ponti in Giornico (Ticino)

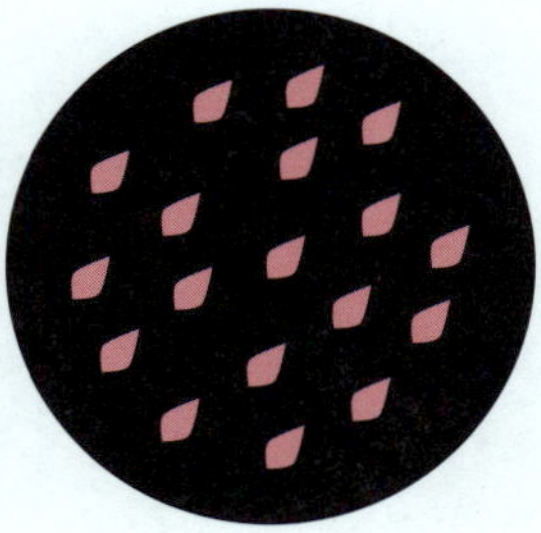

Preparation Time

approx. 4 hours

bake for about 1 hour 10 minutes

Quantity

Makes one round cake.

10-12 servings

INGREDIENTS

Pastry dough

- 300 g (about 6-7 cups) white bread, cut into cubes
- 1 liter (4 ¼ cups) milk
- 100 g (½ cup) sugar
- 100 g (scant 1 cup) amaretti biscuits, crumbled
- 75 g (½ cup) raisins
- 42 g (½ cup) cocoa powder
- 2 eggs
- 45 ml (about 3-4 tablespoons) grappa
- 2 tablespoons all-purpose flour
- 1 teaspoon vanilla paste or extract
- zest of one organic lemon
- 50-60 g (6-7 tablespoons) pine nuts

INSTRUCTIONS

1. Place the bread cubes in a large bowl filled with milk to soak. If the bread is fresh, this will take about 30 minutes. If after this time, the bread is still dry, let it continue to soak for about half a day. When it has softened, use a blender or food processor to blend the bread and milk together. Set aside.

2. Separately, using a blender or food processor to combine the following ingredients: sugar, amaretti, raisins, cocoa powder, eggs, grappa, flour, vanilla and lemon zest. Then, whisk these ingredients together with the bread and milk mixture until well combined.

3. Grease a springform pan with a diameter of about 25 ½-28 cm (10-11 inches) and place a circle of parchment paper on the bottom. Pour in the mixture.

4. Bake for 10 minutes at 240°C / 475°F to form a crust on the surface of the cake. Then, sprinkle the pine nuts evenly on top. Reduce the temperature to 180°C / 350°F and continue baking the cake for about 60 minutes, until a toothpick inserted in the center of the cake comes out free from residue—it should have a moist texture. Let the cake cool in the oven with the door closed.

GROTTO DEI DUE PONTI

A TRADITIONAL BREAD CAKE FROM A TICINESE ISLAND GROTTO

American travel magazine *Travel + Leisure* included Giornico in its 2019 article, "25 Secret European Villages to Explore Before Everyone Else Does." On a rainy summer day, I arrived in this 'secret' Italian-speaking village by bus. My destination? A special grotto found on an island in the middle of the river that carries the same name as the canton, Ticino. This canton is known for having these grotto-style restaurants with typical foods from the region, but this was the first one I had heard of on an island.

A couple got off the bus at the same time I did, and I asked them where they were headed. They mentioned picking up a key at an *osteria* (restaurant) in town. The key would open the door to a gallery with an exhibition of sculptures.

Later I would learn the name of the gallery they were visiting: La Congiunta. This modern concrete building was designed by the architect Peter Märkli and constructed in 1992. Inside, it has a collection of reliefs and sculptures by Zürich artist Hans Josephsohn on display, created between 1950 to 1991. I completely missed this site, instead focusing on other historic landmarks during my visit to Giornico. For a village with fewer than 850 residents, it has a number of fascinating places to discover, nestled in this especially scenic valley.

Not knowing anything at the time about where the couple was headed, I continued on to the Grotto dei Due Ponti ('Grotto of the Two Bridges'), where they eventually ended up as well. We greeted each other when they walked in the door. To reach the grotto, you must traverse one of two Romanesque stone-arched bridges leading to the island. These bridges date back to the 12th and 13th centuries. When you cross the second bridge and reach the other side of the river, you find two particularly sacred structures: San Michele and San Nicola.

A former blacksmith's workshop, the building that houses the Grotto dei Due Ponti was transformed into a restaurant in the 1990s. With grapevines clinging to the arbor over the stone tables of the outdoor terrace, you can listen to the river winding by as you enjoy your meal. I consider it one of those special places that you almost don't want to tell anyone about, for fear of it becoming overrun by tourists.

Seated indoors at the restaurant because of the soaking rain, my main course arrived—a plate with a scoop of grainy yellow polenta, surrounded by six different pieces of local cheese. It was such a simple, rustic dish, but so incredible. For dessert, I ordered a Semifreddo with amaretto. It had piped swirls of whipped cream, five different kinds of fresh fruit artfully placed, sculpted chocolate and a dusting of cocoa powder. At the end of the meal, I had a glass of *nocino*, one of my favorite liqueurs in Switzerland. It gets its flavor from macerated green walnuts (I use this liqueur as an ingredient in my recipe for Crèfli, p. 157). Chef Arturo Sartore has a zero-kilometer goal for his ingredients, a hyper-local approach to creating Ticinese dishes.

A traditional dessert on the menu at the grotto is the Torta di pane. You will find this leftover 'bread cake' throughout Ticino and also across the border in Italy. I like using the cantonal bread for Ticino, Pane ticinese, for this cake. A stale loaf of Einback (p. 27) also works well.

The Torta di pane has many variations, and everyone has their own way of making it. After moistening the bread in milk, you can add a variety of dried fruit (typically raisins, but you can substitute them for cranberries or currants) and nuts (e.g., almonds, pine nuts or walnuts). The addition of dried fruit helps to sweeten the cake, but sugar or honey is also often added to the mixture. Crumbled Amaretti biscuits, which the recipe from Grotto dei Due Ponti calls for, also add a nice flavor to the cake, if you have some left over. Bakers will traditionally add an egg to help bind all these ingredients together.

This old recipe can also be appreciated today for helping to use up stale bread, and therefore reducing food waste. I especially enjoy Torta di pane for breakfast with some coffee or for an afternoon snack with a cup of tea. Wait a day before you cut into this rich cake though, giving its flavors more time to develop.

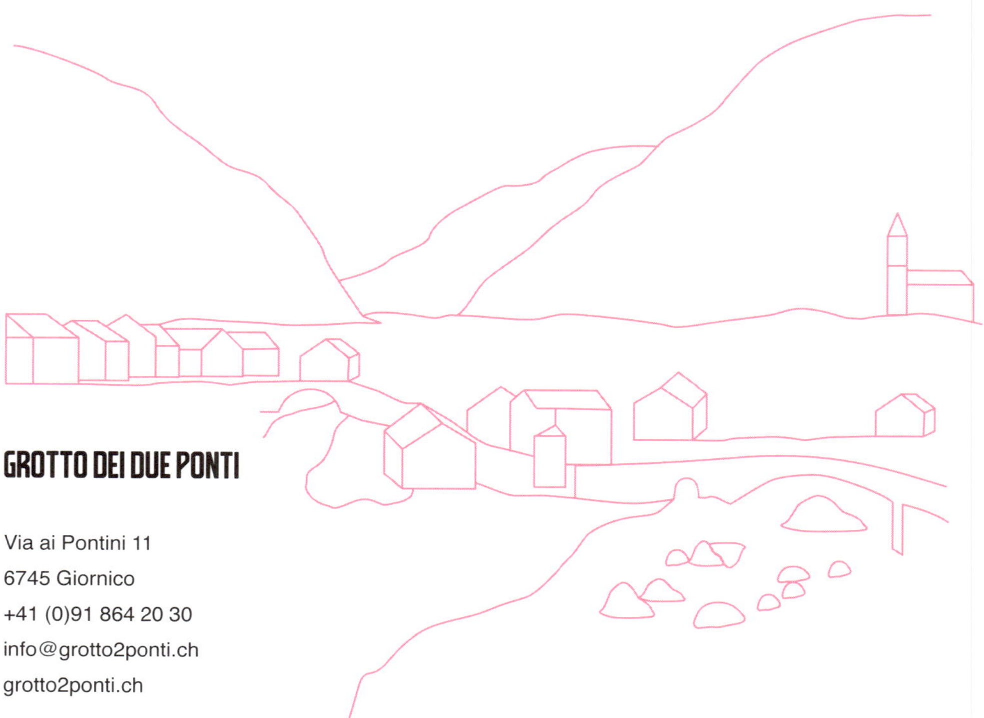

GROTTO DEI DUE PONTI

Via ai Pontini 11
6745 Giornico
+41 (0)91 864 20 30
info@grotto2ponti.ch
grotto2ponti.ch

15 FIDERISER TORTE

Preparation Time
approx. 1 hour 30 minutes
bake for 20-25 minutes

Quantity
Makes one cake.
8-10 servings

INGREDIENTS

Dough:

- 100 g (7 tablespoons) unsalted butter, softened
- 100 g (½ cup) sugar
- 1 egg
- 100 g (1 ¼ cups) ground almonds or hazelnuts
- 175 g (1 ⅓ cups + 1 tablespoon) all-purpose flour
- 1 teaspoon cinnamon
- ½ teaspoon baking soda
- ¼ teaspoon salt

Filling:

- 150 g (approx. ½ cup) raspberry jam (or another type of jam)

Brush on before baking:

- 1 egg, beaten

INSTRUCTIONS

1. Combine the butter, sugar and egg together in a large bowl until it becomes a smooth mixture. Stir in the ground almonds.

2. In a separate bowl, whisk together the remaining dough ingredients: all-purpose flour, cinnamon, baking soda and salt.

3. Add the dry ingredients to the wet ingredients in the large bowl. Stir together just until a dough forms. Divide the dough into two pieces, with one being slightly larger. Flatten them into disks by hand and chill them in the refrigerator for approximately 60 minutes.

4. Grease a non-stick tart pan with a diameter of about 24 cm (9 ½ inches) with butter or line it with parchment paper. When the dough is ready, remove it from the refrigerator. Start with the large disk of dough. Place it on parchment paper or a surface lightly dusted with flour. Using a rolling pin also lightly dusted with flour, roll out the dough to create the bottom layer of the cake—make the circle larger than the diameter of the pan. Invert the parchment paper over the prepared pan and gently peel it away from the dough. Press the dough into the pan, pressing the dough just slightly up the sides of the pan.

5. Prick the bottom of the dough (not the sides) all around with a fork, to prevent air pockets from forming. Spread the jam evenly over the bottom layer. Then, roll out the second piece

of dough to fit the diameter of the pan, as described in step 4. Gently place it over the jam and brush the beaten egg on the surface of the cake. Next, use a fork to press down the outer edge of the dough. Finally, drag the fork across the surface of the dough to create a lattice pattern.

6. Bake at 180˚C / 350°F for 20-25 minutes, until the surface of the cake has lightly browned. After 10 minutes, remove the cake from the pan, carefully loosening the sides, and place on a wire rack to cool.

A LEGENDARY LINZER-ESQUE CAKE WITH A POTENTIAL RUSSIAN CONNECTION

Once again in Graubünden, one of my favorite Swiss cantons, I found myself on a pastry chase. This time, on my way home from Pontresina, I stopped in the tiny village of Fideris on a mission to taste its eponymous cake. It had been on my bucket list for years.

A village with about 600 people, located at an elevation of 900 meters above sea level in the Prättigau region, Fideris is known for its Fideriser Torte. Similar to the Austrian Linzertorte, this sandwich cake has two nutty biscuit layers with a jam filling, typically raspberry. In Switzerland, the St. Galler Klostertorte most resembles the Fideriser Torte. It contains cocoa or chocolate powder in the dough, however, giving the pastry a deep-brown color. Furthermore, unlike the Linzertorte and the Klostertorte, which have lattice lids that expose the jam within, the Fideriser Torte has a solid lid. Without having to weave the dough into a criss-crossed pattern, I think the Fideriser Torte is easier to make for home bakers than the St. Galler Klostertorte or the Linzertorte.

The legend of the Fideriser Torte begins with the Bad Fideris ('baths'). The first mention of these baths, where people went for relaxation and to try and improve their health, dates back to 1464. Centuries later, a man named Ulrich Boner worked at Bad Fideris baking sweet treats for the guests. According to the local legend, after having spent time working as a pastry chef in Russia, he returned to Switzerland with a cake recipe that he was making at the end of the 19th century at the baths. Eventually, his recipe ended up at the Gujan bakery in Fideris around the year 1900. The bakery uses ground almonds in its cake, but recipes exist with ground hazelnuts as well. For example, in Marianne Kaltenbach's book, *Ächti Schwizer Chuchi* ('Real Swiss Cuisine', 1977), she uses almonds and also adds rosewater to the dough, while other recipes might use kirsch instead.

The Gujan bakery remains, as does the cake, where the fourth generation of this family still makes it. You can find it at the bakery year-round, but it is particularly popular during the Christmas season.

Fast forward to my visit to this quiet village, where its famous baths closed in the 1930s. After the bus dropped me off by the schoolhouse, I walked up the street and found a wooden sign that read, *Bäckerei,* with an arrow pointing to the left. With a slight downward gradient, I followed the village road and found the small bakery on the corner. In the window, a large Fideriser Torte was on display. I eagerly stepped in to pick up a white box filled with this special round cake to take home to my family.

When you enjoy the Fideriser Torte, for breakfast with coffee or during the holiday season with your family and friends, you can imagine this quiet village with its legend of a Russian sojourn that led to a piece of Switzerland's culinary heritage.

Bad Fideris (Fideriser baths) in the early 19th century.
Inspired by an illustration from the 1830s by David Alois Schmid and Kaspar Burkhard; held by the Swiss National Library.

16 CHOCOLATE GUGELHOPF

Preparation Time

approx. 30 minutes

bake for 40-50 minutes

Quantity

Makes one cake.

8-10 servings

INGREDIENTS

Cake:

- 225 g (1 ¾ cups) all-purpose flour
- 1 tablespoon cocoa powder
- ¾ teaspoon baking powder
- ¼ teaspoon baking soda
- ¼ teaspoon salt
- 225 g (1 cup) unsalted butter
- 225 g (1 cup + 2 tablespoons) sugar
- 50 g (3 tablespoons + 1 teaspoon) yogurt
- 1 teaspoon vanilla sugar or extract
- 2 eggs
- 200 g (7 oz) dark chocolate
- 250 ml (1 cup) milk

Glaze (optional):

- 100 g (scant ¾ cup) powdered sugar
- 2-3 tablespoons water

INSTRUCTIONS

1. Prepare a Gugelhopf or Bundt pan (size: 10 cups / 2.3 liters). First, grease the pan generously with butter and then lightly dust it with flour. Tap the pan to remove excess flour. Set aside.

2. Sift the flour, cocoa powder, baking powder, baking soda and salt into a large bowl. Whisk together until well combined. Set aside.

3. Break up the chocolate into smaller squares and add it to a heat-safe bowl. Place the bowl over a water bath (bain-marie), stirring occasionally, until all the chocolate is melted. Set aside to cool.

4. While the chocolate is cooling, cream together butter, sugar, yogurt and vanilla together until well combined. Then, beat in the eggs, one at a time, until the mixture becomes light and fluffy.

5. Stir the chocolate into the butter-sugar mixture until it's completely incorporated.

6. Finally, add the flour mixture and milk, in two batches, stirring just until all the ingredients are incorporated into the batter.

7. Pour batter into the prepared cake pan. Bake for 40-50 minutes at 180°C / 350°F. To test if the cake is done, insert a toothpick or skewer, and if it comes out clean, take the cake out of the oven. Let the cake cool in the pan for about 10 minutes, and then carefully remove from the pan. Place on a wire rack to cool completely.

Serving suggestions: (1) dust the cake with some powdered sugar (2) whisk together the ingredients for my glaze recipe and pour it over the cake when it has completely cooled or (3) serve it with a dollop of whipped cream and seasonal fruit.

A CLASSIC SWISS DARK CHOCOLATE CAKE WITH A HOLE IN ITS MIDDLE

The governor of the state of Minnesota declared November 15, 2006, as National Bundt Day to mark the 60th anniversary of this popular cake pan. Created by the Nordic Ware company, which has its headquarters in my home state, the Bundt cake is the American version of the Gugelhopf (also known as Gugelhupf or Kugelhopf) in Switzerland.

I have always had a particular affinity for a fluted cake with a hole in its center. One year, I baked three Bundt cakes in a day to celebrate this 'holiday' that started in Minnesota. My sister and I, rarely in the same place on this day, send photos back and forth of the cakes we are making. One of my favorite photos that she took comes from the Minnesota State Fair. It shows rows of enticing Bundt cakes entered in the fair's annual baking competition.

When I arrived in Switzerland, I started seeing Gugelhopf cakes around the country. I noticed packets of baking powder at the supermarkets with an image of a Gugelhopf on them. A common type of Swiss Gugelhopf, I learned, is a *marmor* ('marble') version that involves a chocolate cake batter swirled with a vanilla batter. Then, at the Confiserie Sprüngli location at Zürich's main train station, I saw one of the most exquisite types of these cakes—a chocolate Gugelhopf coated in a rich chocolate icing. Further research led me to Basel, where I bought the yeasted version of these cakes, a Hefegugelhopf.

What I love about the Gugelhopf is that the pan does all the work. You don't have to fuss with lots of decoration. Just sprinkle some powdered sugar on top, and it will look great. One of my favorite Swiss-inspired recipes is my Absinthe Gugelhopf—a recipe I published on my blog.

To make sure the cake does not get stuck in the pan, I first coat every corner of the pan with butter and then dust it with flour. Make sure to tap the inverted pan to remove any excess flour. Others may use ground nuts or cocoa powder instead of flour. Everyone has their own preferences, so do what works best for you and your pan. And if your cake doesn't come out perfectly, a glaze will usually cover minor (and even more major) imperfections.

My inspiration for this recipe comes from a Swiss chocolate cake sometimes referred to as the Lützelflüher Schokoladentorte or the Gotthelftorte. Lützelflüh is a town in the Emmental district, located within the canton of Bern. It also happens to be where a well-known Swiss German writer used to serve as a pastor. Born Albert Bitzius in 1797, he eventually became known under the pseudonym Jeremias Gotthelf. His writing focused on the agrarian way of life in this region of Switzerland. Morality tales feature heavily in his body of work, which includes over a dozen novels and no fewer than 50 short stories. *Die schwarze Spinne* ('The Black Spider') is one of his best-known books, which depicts a town besieged by spiders when one of its community members breaks a pact made with the devil.

At this point, you may be wondering what Gotthelf has to do with a chocolate cake? The recipes I have seen in various cookbooks and online often point to his daughter as the source. It was supposedly the family recipe for birthday cakes, although not made in the Gugelhopf form as I have done. Swiss cookbook author Annemarie Wildeisen published a recipe for this cake in her 2011 book, *Heissgeliebtes Backen*. She wrote that it came from a cookbook prepared by Gotthelf's daughter, which somehow came into her family's possession over the years. This recipe, like the others for this cake, generally contains equal parts butter, sugar, flour and chocolate.

My version of the Gotthelf family cake has a little plain yogurt added to the batter to help moisten its texture. When drizzled with a powdered sugar glaze, it reminds me a bit of an American chocolate cake doughnut. At Christmas time, I use a Gugelhopf pan ringed with pine trees. Sprinkled with crushed American candy canes, it has become an annual tradition in my household, albeit a little different than Gotthelf's daughter's cake.

17 TUORTA DA NUSCHS

Preparation Time
approx. 2 hours 30 minutes
bake for 30-40 minutes

Quantity
Makes one cake.
8-10 servings

INGREDIENTS

Dough:

- 250 g (2 cups) all-purpose flour
- 75 g (½ cup) powdered sugar
- ¼ teaspoon salt
- 125 g (9 tablespoons) unsalted butter, cold
- 1 egg, lightly beaten

Filling:

- 200 ml (¾ cup + 1 ½ tablespoons) heavy cream (35% milk fat)
- 1 tablespoon honey
- 1 teaspoon vanilla extract or paste
- ¼ teaspoon salt
- 200 g (1 cup) sugar
- 1 tablespoon water
- 1 teaspoon lemon juice
- 200 g (2 cups) walnuts, chopped

Topping:

- 1 egg, beaten

INSTRUCTIONS

Pastry dough

1. In a large bowl, whisk together the all-purpose flour, powdered sugar and salt until well combined. Add the butter, in pieces to the bowl and then use your fingers or a pastry blender to mix in the butter with the dry ingredients until it become the size of small pebbles. Next, form a well in the center of the bowl and add the lightly beaten egg. Stir the mixture together just until a dough forms. Add 1-2 tbsp water if needed. Wrap the dough in parchment paper and place it in the refrigerator for about 30-60 minutes.

2. When the dough has chilled, grease a rectangular tart pan with a removable bottom (size: 10 x 35 cm / 4 x 14 inches) with butter. Take about two-third of the dough and roll it out on a piece of parchment paper. Using a rolling pin, lightly dusted with flour, roll out the dough to a thickness of about 3 mm (1⁄10 of an inch) to fit the springform pan. Invert the parchment paper and dough over the pan, and gently peel back the paper and press the dough into the pan to fit the bottom and sides of the pan. Trim any excess dough. Prick the bottom of the dough in the pan with a fork and place the springform pan in the refrigerator to chill the dough again.

3. Now prepare the lattice top. Roll out the remaining dough on a lightly floured surface, again with a thickness of about 3 mm (1⁄10 of an inch. Using a pastry wheel or a sharp knife, cut strips into the dough with a width about 1 to 2 cm (½ to ¾ of an inch). On a baking sheet lined with parchment paper, make a lattice crust to fit the size and shape of the pan, weaving the dough strips together. When you finish, place the lattice in the fridge to cool along with the dough in the springform pan.

Caramel-walnut filling

4. With the dough chilling in the fridge, start-preparing the filling. First, whisk together the heavy cream, honey, vanilla and salt. Set aside.

5. Then, add the sugar, water and lemon juice to a medium saucepan. Do not stir them together. Over low to medium heat, gently start heating and caramelizing the sugar, so it turns a golden brown. Watch the pan almost constantly, because sugar can burn quickly. Instead of stirring, tilt the pan slightly from time to time, so the contents of the pan move around, and the sugar can caramelize evenly. Be patient – this process can take about 30 minutes.

6. When the sugar mixture has developed a deep golden-brown color, take the pan off the burner and slowly add the cream mixture in a thin stream, whisking as it gets added to the pan. When the cream mixture has been fully incorporated into the caramelized sugar, return the pan to the burner, and continue to simmer the mixture over medium-low heat. Once the mixture begins to bubble and thicken, so that you can see the bottom of the pan when you stir it with a spoon or whisk, take it off the heat and stir in the chopped walnuts. Let this mixture cool and thicken.

Assembling the tart

7. At this time, turn on the oven to 180°C / 350°F. Beat an egg in a small bowl and set aside. Take the springform pan out of the fridge and pour in the caramel-walnut filling. Then, remove the dough lattice from the fridge and invert the piece of parchment with the dough onto the surface of the springform pan. Remove any excess dough from the sides of the pan and make sure the lattice design extends across the entire surface of the filling. Then, brush the beaten egg on the surface of the lattice topping. Bake at the bottom of the oven for 30-40 minutes, until the filling is bubbling and the pastry has developed a light golden-brown color.

8. Let the tart cool in the pan for about 10-15 minutes. Then, remove the tart from the pan and let it cool completely on a wire rack. To store the cake, wrap it tightly in aluminum foil.

GRAUBÜNDEN'S FAMOUS CARAMEL-WALNUT CAKE

"Nine months of winter and three months of cold," is something the locals say to describe the weather in the Engadin Valley of Graubünden. With relatively cold temperatures throughout the year, the culinary specialties from this alpine region have quite a hearty reputation. Many local dishes are made to last, especially during the long winter months. The Tuorta da nuschs (Romansh) or Nusstorte (German) is an example of a sweet specialty that fits this category of long-lasting foods. Bakers wrap a sweet short crust pastry around a rich caramel and walnut filling. Both professional and home bakers make this walnut cake, which reminds me a bit of an American pecan pie.

The Nusstorte does not have a clear origin story, but for several reasons, people have theorized that the recipe came from outside of Switzerland. First, walnuts have not been historically grown in the cool alpine climate of Graubünden. Second, this Swiss canton was known for having talented pastry chefs during the 17th century. Many left to pursue professional opportunities in Italy and France, and then returned to the region with new recipes and culinary influences. This departure occurred in particular around 1630, as Venice welcomed these talented workers following a period of the plague. Eventually, after political conflicts with the city of Chur, Venice expelled its Swiss pastry chefs, who took their baking talents elsewhere, particularly to France.

In France, one cake has especially been cited as an inspiration for the Swiss Nusstorte. The Heinz & Tester bakery, which employed Bündner confectioners, baked a Gâteau aux noix ('walnut cake') between the period of 1881 to 1930, according to research compiled by Swiss culinary historian Paul Imhof for graubündenVIVA. Fausto Pult worked at this French address and eventually opened his own shop in Samedan in 1926. While some claim he brought the recipe with him from Paris, his descendents say it was a family recipe. You can still purchase this walnut cake made with the original recipe from Laager's bakery in Samedan.

Separately, another bakery in Graubünden started selling a walnut cake commercially in the early 20th century, Konditorei Ribi in Chur. Adolf Ribi, who also worked in Paris, opened his shop in 1901. According to a family member, these cakes were even sent to the United States because of their long shelf life. It is no longer in operation, but some claim this bakery as the birthplace of the Nusstorte in Switzerland.

Regardless of where it came from, the Nusstorte has become fully rooted in the culinary heritage of Graubünden and the nation. Today, you can find different types of these walnut cakes in bakeries and supermarkets throughout the country. The pastry dough used to make it resembles the large round biscuit, also from this region, known as the Fuatscha grassa.

One year during a visit to Scuol in the Engadin, I went in search of the best Nusstorte in town. At various shops and the tourist office, I asked for recommendations and then tested four of them myself. Everyone I talked to had their favorite place to go, and for different reasons. To my surprise, someone who grew up in this area told me to visit a local Swiss supermarket chain in town. A home-based baker sold her tinfoil-wrapped cake at the store. Compared to some of the others I had tried, it had a larger proportion of filling and a slightly thinner pastry. It tasted homemade, but in the best way. Another baker from this area makes his in an attractive, but non-standard triangular shape. There are so many variations of this cake, and now I'm adding my version to the mix with an atypical lattice design on top.

With my recipe, I wanted to showcase the filling, instead of covering it completely with a solid lid. Of course, the original intent of the dough-encased filling had a practical reason—to help the cake stay fresher for longer. With the exposed caramel-walnut filling, my version reminds me more of a tart than a cake. I like to slice it into small pieces and serve with coffee or tea to cut the sweetness of this rich dessert.

18 VEGAN RÜEBLITORTE

from Zineb Hattab, Restaurant KLE in Zürich (Zürich)

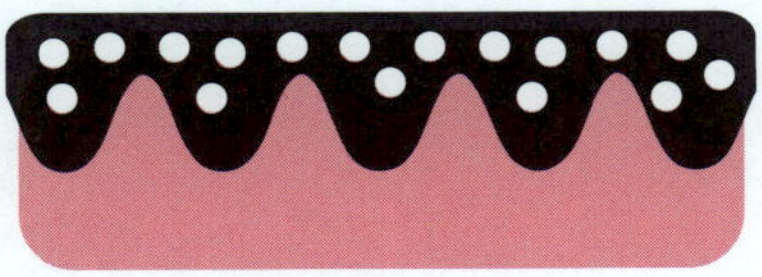

Preparation Time

approx. 30 minutes

bake for 35-40 minutes

Quantity

Makes one cake.

8-10 servings

INGREDIENTS

Dry ingredients:

- 250 g (2 cups) all-purpose flour
- 1 teaspoon cinnamon
- ¾ teaspoon baking soda
- ½ teaspoon salt
- ¼ teaspoon nutmeg
- ¼ teaspoon ground ginger
- a pinch of ground cloves

Wet ingredients:

- 250 g (2 ⅓ cups) finely grated carrots
- 150 ml (⅔ cup) water
- 125 g (⅔ cup) raw cane sugar
- 100 ml (⅓ cup + 2 tablespoons) olive oil
- 15 ml (about 1 tablespoon) apple cider vinegar
- 1 teaspoon vanilla extract or paste

White chocolate frosting:

- 75 g (2 ⅔ oz) vegan white chocolate, finely chopped
- 150 ml (⅔ cup) plant-based whipping cream (e.g., soy or almond)

INSTRUCTIONS

Pastry dough

1. Prepare a cake pan with a diameter of about 24 cm (9 ½ inches). Add a small drop of oil to the bottom and sides and line it with parchment paper. Set aside.

2. In a large bowl, whisk together the dry ingredients: all-purpose flour, cinnamon, baking soda, salt, nutmeg, ginger and cloves. Set aside.

3. In another large bowl, stir together the wet ingredients until well combined: finely grated carrots, water, raw cane sugar, olive oil, apple cider vinegar and vanilla.

4. Slowly add the dry ingredients to the wet ingredients, stirring just until the flour is absorbed and completely incorporated into the mixture.

5. Pour and spread the batter evenly into the prepared cake pan. Bake for about 35-40 minutes at 180˚C / 350°F. To test if the cake is done, insert a toothpick or skewer into the center, and if it comes out clean, without any crumbs stuck to it, take the cake out of the oven.

6. Let the cake cool in the pan for about 10 minutes and then transfer onto a wire rack.

7. When the cake has completely cooled, make the frosting. Place the finely chopped chocolate into a heat-proof bowl. Next, heat the plant-based whipping cream in a medium saucepan just until boiling. Then, remove it from the heat and pour half of it over the chocolate. Whisk the chocolate together with the warmed cream so that it begins to melt and add the remaining cream, stirring until the mixture is well combined. Place the mixture in the refrigerator to cool for several hours, so that it becomes thick enough to spread on the cooled cake. Then, use an electric mixer to whip the frosting until it is thick and spreadable.

8. When the frosting is ready, spread it on the top of the carrot cake.

Optional: Decorate the cake with candied walnuts (p. 221) or crumbled speculoos biscuits.

Weststrasse
KLE

A VEGAN CARROT CAKE FOR SWITZERLAND

Zineb 'Zizi' Hattab grew up with her Moroccan parents in Spain, surrounded by family. She has fond memories of making strawberry sponge cakes with her father when she was young. Now in Zürich, most recently via New York City, she leads the kitchen at one the city's most innovative and exciting restaurants. She has zero regrets about her last-minute decision to offer an entirely plant-based menu at her Restaurant KLE. Its name derives from *sauerklee*, the German word for wood sorrel. The menu at KLE has a wonderful vegan carrot cake with creamy white chocolate frosting, which could be considered a reinterpretation of a classic Swiss cake.

Switzerland has a long history of making carrot cakes, a recipe typically associated with Aargau. This canton is the supposed home of the Swiss carrot cake because of its reputation for growing copious amounts of this pointy, orange-hued vegetable. The legend has stuck with Aargau over the years, even though other cantons now actually grow more carrots. Sometimes referred to as Rüebliland, a name thought to have started in the late 19th century, there are apparently at least four theories as to what led to its image as a carrot-growing region. One popular story involves a priest from Basel who worked in Brugg and brought some local carrots home to his family.

You will also find a special kind of carrot grown in this region called the *küttiger rüebli*. This ivory-colored vegetable is part of the inventory of Patrimoine Culinaire Suisse and is recognized as an heirloom variety by ProSpecieRara. Today the canton has embraced its reputation as Switzerland's carrot capital, increasing the acreage where carrots are grown and hosting an annual *rüeblimarkt* (carrot market), on the first Wednesday in November.

At her restaurant, Zineb has created a new vegan approach to this classic Swiss cake. With her recipe, she carries on the tradition of the famous Aargauer Rüeblitorte, but with plant-based ingredients. Her cake also has an American influence, inspired by the moist and thickly frosted versions in the US, picked up during Hattab's time at Cosme restaurant in New York City.

Hattab's Restaurant KLE in Zürich's Wiedikon neighborhood opened in January 2020. Within months of its opening, while in the final preparation phase for her restaurant, she abruptly decided to stop eating animal products. In describing to me what a sudden change it was, she said her fridge had nearly two kilograms of cheese in it when she decided to go vegan. Her husband thought she was crazy.

What drove her to make this rapid change? With the launch of her first restaurant, she started asking herself, “What do I bring to the table? Am I just another nice restaurant to go to? What is missing? How can I really have an impact?" She decided to make what some might consider a drastic move, cutting out all animal products from her diet, as well as from her new restaurant's menu. Her motives are connected to promoting sustainability, improving personal health and protecting animal welfare. In 2021, she opened a second plant-based restaurant with Spanish and Moroccan influences named DAR.

Zineb likes desserts (and French fries), and she used to make a lot of Bündner Nusstortes when she worked for the three-starred Michelin chef Chef Andreas Caminada at Schloss Schauenstein in Graubünden. I asked her about how she approaches recipe development now that she's making plant-based desserts. She said, "When I make an ice cream, whipped cream or a meringue, it's very different because these are usually made with animal proteins." She must think about the chemistry behind a particular dish by asking the question, "What is the transformation that I'm looking for?" For example, when she makes ice cream, she uses a plant-based milk which has a lower percentage of fat, so she needs to add other ingredients to increase the fat percentage to more like 15-20%, similar to what whole milk would have. The former software engineer said, "It's not about looking at what you don't have, but understanding what you're doing. It's like if you try to write something in German with Spanish words, it's not going to work."

This sense of problem-solving and creativity helps Hattab to develop her vegan recipes, such as her luscious carrot cake with a creamy white chocolate topping. While familiar with the Swiss carrot cake—an often gluten-free cake made with egg whites and ground almonds or hazelnuts (I have a recipe on my blog)—she prefers an American-style cake with a softer, moist texture. Drawing on more Spanish and Italian traditions, she uses olive oil to add fat to the batter. Her frosting does not contain cream cheese, but instead calls for a vegan white chocolate ganache. Whether you order this cake at KLE or make it at home, you will not miss the milk and eggs in this light and decadent, spiced vegetable cake. With recipes like this, she symbolizes a new era of Swiss chefs establishing a more sustainable paradigm for the world of gastronomy.

RESTAURANT KLE

Zweierstrasse 114
8003 Zürich
+41 (0)44 548 14 88
info@restaurantkle.com
restaurantkle.com

19 ZIMTFLADEN

Preparation Time

approx. 2 hours
bake for 25-30 minutes

Quantity

Makes one tart.
8-10 servings

INGREDIENTS

Dough:

- 125 g (1 cup) all-purpose flour
- 75 g (½ cup) whole wheat flour
- ¼ teaspoon salt
- 75 g (⅓ cup) unsalted butter, cold
- 1 egg
- 50 ml (¼ cup) water, cold

Filling:

- 3 tablespoons raspberry jam (or currant, apricot, etc.)
- 150 grams (¾ cup) sugar
- 42 grams (2 tablespoons) honey
- 2 eggs
- 75 g (½ cup + 1 tablespoon) all-purpose flour
- 75 g (⅔ cup) whole wheat flour
- 1 tablespoon cinnamon
- 1 teaspoon baking powder
- ½ teaspoon ground coriander
- ¼ teaspoon ground cloves
- ¼ teaspoon salt
- 250 ml (2 cups) light cream (25% milk fat)

INSTRUCTIONS

1. First make the pastry. Whisk the white and whole wheat flours together with the salt in a large bowl. Add the cold butter, in pieces. Using a food processor, pastry blender or two knives, cut the butter pieces into the flour mixture, until it becomes the size of small pebbles. Make a well in the center of the mixture and add the egg and cold water. Stir together until a dough forms. Shape the dough into a disk and refrigerate it for about 30-60 minutes.

2. Line a tart pan with a diameter of about 30 cm (11 ½ inches) with parchment paper. Take the dough out of the fridge and roll it out on a lightly floured surface. Place it into the prepared tart pan. Using a fork, prick the bottom of the dough. Then, spread the jam evenly on the bottom of the dough. Place the pan with the dough back in the fridge to cool.

3. Make the cake batter. In a large bowl, whisk the sugar, honey and eggs together until the mixture becomes a bit foamy. Sift the dry ingredients: the flours, spices, baking powder and salt. Add the sifted mixture and the cream, alternating these ingredients, to the egg mixture in the large bowl and stir until they have become completely incorporated, creating a smooth cake batter.

4. Take the pan with the dough and raspberry jam out of the fridge. Pour the cake batter evenly into the pan. Bake the tart on the bottom rack of the oven for about 25-30 minutes at 200°C / 400°F. Let it rest in the pan for about 10 minutes. Then, remove the cake from the pan and place it on a wire rack to cool.

A CINNAMON 'PAKE' FROM EASTERN SWITZERLAND

The Zimtfladen comes from the cantons of Appenzell (Ausserrhoden and Innerrhoden), as well as the Toggenburg region of St. Gallen. I had been making this gently sweet dessert for years, when someone pointed out via Instagram that it could be considered a 'pake' (pie + cake).

Switzerland has another pake-like sweet treat, known as the Studentenschnitten. To make it, bakers first brush a short crust pastry with jam. Then, they add a cake batter, often chocolate, which typically contains leftover cookies. Before cutting them into rectangular pieces, an icing is spread on their surface. Once again, bakers often use a chocolate icing for this purpose. These treats are solid and filling, and as their name implies, a snack intended for students.

Like the Studentenschnitten, the Zimtfladen also has a layer of jam applied before bakers add the cinnamon-scented cake batter. Not only made with cinnamon, the mixture of spices in this tart resembles gingerbread. Its name has the famous suffix *-fladen* from Eastern Switzerland that means a round, flat bread or cake. You will find a similar use of this term for the dried pear tart called the Schlorzifladen (p. 129). The Zimtfladen typically has a short crust pastry, but you can also make it with puff pastry.

In the city of St. Gallen, I have read that one of the best Zimtfladen can be found at the Milchhüsli-Imbiss. Located above the city center in an area known as Dreilinden (or Drei Weihern, 'three ponds'), this seasonal snack bar for swimmers is apparently the place to go. While you are there, I also recommend having a St. Galler Bratwurst and Bürli bread roll.

For my recipe, I have created a somewhat heartier Zimtfladen by adding whole wheat flour to the pastry, as well as to the cake batter. A lightly sweetened cake, it tastes good on its own, or perhaps even for breakfast. One of my favorite ways to serve it is with a generous dollop of whipped cream.

20 FLON DE SAVIÈSE

Preparation Time

approx. 1 hour 30 minutes
bake for 35-45 minutes

Quantity

Makes one tart.
8-10 servings

INGREDIENTS

Dough:

- 125 g (1 cup) all-purpose flour
- 75 g (⅔ cup) whole wheat flour
- ¼ teaspoon salt
- 75 g (⅓ cup) unsalted butter, cold
- 1 egg
- 1-2 tablespoons water, cold

Crumble:

- 125 g (⅔ cup) sugar
- 100 g (¾ cup) all-purpose flour
- 1 teaspoon cinnamon
- 100 g (½ cup + 2 tablespoons) unsalted butter, cold
- a pinch of salt

Apples:

- juice of one lemon
- 1 to 1 ¼ kg (2 ¼ to 2 ¾ lbs) apples for baking

INSTRUCTIONS

Dough

1. Make the dough. Whisk the all-purpose flour, wheat flour and salt together in a large bowl. Add the cold butter in pieces. Make a well in the middle of the mixture. Add the egg and 1-2 tablespoons of water. Stir the mixture together just until a dough forms. Wrap in parchment paper and refrigerate for about 30-60 minutes.

2. When the dough is ready, grease a non-stick round tart pan or line it with parchment paper (diameter: 28 cm, 11 inches). Roll out the dough on the sheet of parchment paper it was wrapped in. Make it into a circle large enough to fit the pan and invert the paper over the pan. Peel off the parchment paper and trim excess dough. Prick the bottom of the dough with a fork, and place the pan in the fridge to chill for a second time.

Crumble

3. Prepare the crumble. In a large bowl, whisk together the flour, sugar, cinnamon and salt. Add the cold butter, in pieces, to the bowl. Using your hands, break down the butter, forming it into small pebble-sized pieces. The pieces of butter should be well distributed, and the mixture should have a sandy, crumbly texture. Set aside.

Apples

4. Add the juice from one lemon to a large bowl. Peel and core the apples, cut them into thin slices, and add them immediately to the large bowl. Gently toss the apples in the bowl with your hands, coating them in the lemon juice to prevent them from turning brown.

5. Once all the apples are ready, take the tart pan out of the fridge with the prepared dough. Sprinkle about two-thirds of the crumble mixture evenly in the bottom of the pan. Then, lift the apples out of the large bowl, leaving any excess juice, and place them evenly into the pan on top of the crumble mixture. After that, sprinkle the remaining one-third of the crumble evenly over the fresh apples.

6. Bake the tart at 180°C / 350°F for about 35-45 minutes, until the apples have softened and the crumbled and pastry has turned a light golden brown. Let the tart cool slightly, or completely, before serving.

AN APPLE TART FROM VALAIS WITH A 'CRUMBLE' TOPPING

In the canton of Valais, the Savièse region includes over a dozen villages along the hillside above the capital city of Sion. A special fruit tart takes the name of this region. The Chavyejan (Saviésans in the local dialect) have been making it since at least the 1950s. I first stumbled across the Flon de Savièse in Sion. On vacation with my family, I stepped into the Boulangerie Gaillard & Fils in search of sandwiches and pastries. The rectangular slice of a fruit tart had a *sablé-sucré* topping, which I would best describe as a 'crumble.' I had seen tarts like this before, but this one has the crumble sprinkled both under and over the fruit.

Not to be confused with the savory Tarte savièsanne, which contains potatoes, leeks and cheese wrapped in pastry, the sweet Flon de Savièse is often made with apples. You will also frequently see them with stone fruits, such as apricots and plums. In this region, the local patois term *flon* refers to a tart, similar to how the Swiss Germans in Eastern Switzerland use the suffix *-fladen* for flat, round cakes (see p. 129 for the Schlorzifladen and p. 111 for the Zimtfladen). The crumble topping is simply a combination of butter, flour and sugar, with some bakers adding cinnamon, like I do. It has a tradition in home kitchens, but as demonstrated in Sion, professional bakers also still make it.

It seems the Flon de Savièse has a bit of a reputation for being a retro dish, most likely made by a grandmother. Journalist Melina Schröter wrote passionately on the subject of preserving these old recipes in a 2016 article (translated from French) that appeared in the daily newspaper, *Le Matin.*

> "... when our grandmothers will no longer be there to cook bricelets and flons de Savièse, when no craftsman will offer *papet vaudois* and *atriaux* any more, when standardized stores will have replaced the small neighborhood bars, our heritage will have lost part of its know-how and, dare we say it, its soul." Melina Schröter, for lematin.ch (October 8, 2016)

As I write this, the hashtag #flondesavièse on Instagram is found on only one post, published under my account, @cuisinehelvetica. Would you please help me promote this wonderful Swiss French fruit tart? When you make it at home or buy it from a local bakery, you help maintain one of Switzerland's culinary traditions. I'll be looking for your photos! Plus, most importantly, with its tender baked apples and the sandy texture of its sweet *sablé*, this tart just simply tastes so good.

21 GÂTEAU AUX NOISETTES

Preparation Time

approx. 1 hour

bake for 30-40 minutes

Quantity

Makes one tart.

8-10 servings

INGREDIENTS

Dough:

- 125 g (1 cup) all-purpose flour
- 75 g (²⁄₃ cup) whole wheat flour
- ¼ teaspoon salt
- 75 g (⅓ cup) unsalted butter, cold
- 1 egg
- 1-2 tablespoons water, cold

Filling:

- about 2 tablespoons apricot jam (optional)
- 1 egg yolk
- 50 g (¼ cup) sugar
- 200 g (2 ½ cups) ground hazelnuts (or almonds)
- 200 ml (¾ cup + 1 ½ tablespoons) heavy cream (35% milk fat)
- 1-2 teaspoons vanilla extract or paste
- zest of half an organic lemon
- 2 egg whites
- a pinch of salt

Icing:

- 100 g (¾ cup + 2 tablespoons) powdered sugar
- 1-2 tablespoons water

INSTRUCTIONS

Dough

1. First make the pastry. Whisk the white and whole wheat flours together with the salt in a large bowl. Add the cold butter, in pieces. Using a food processor, pastry blender or two knives, cut the butter into the flour mixture, until it becomes the size of small pebbles. Make a well in the center of the mixture and add the egg and cold water. Stir together until dough forms. Shape the dough into a disk and refrigerate the dough for about 30-60 minutes, so it becomes firm.

2. While the dough is chilling, toast the ground hazelnuts. Place them on a baking sheet lined with parchment paper. Place the pan in an oven heated to 180°C / 350° F and toast the nuts for 5-10 minutes, keeping an eye on them so they don't burn. Let the nuts fully cool before adding them to the filling.

3. When the dough has chilled, line a tart pan with a diameter of about 30 cm (11 ½ inches) with parchment paper. Take the dough out of the fridge and roll it out on a lightly floured surface.

Place it into the prepared tart pan. Using a fork, prick the bottom of the dough. Then, spread the jam evenly on the bottom of the dough (optional). Place the pan with the dough back in the fridge to cool for another 15 minutes.

4. While the dough is re-chilling, add the egg yolk and sugar to a large bowl or an electric mixer and blend until the mixture begins to lighten in color to a pale yellow. Then stir in the toasted ground hazelnuts, cream, vanilla and lemon zest until well combined. Set aside.

5. Separately, use an electric mixer or a whisk to whip the egg whites together with a pinch of salt until they become fluffy and form stiff peaks. Then, gently fold them into the hazelnut mixture in the large bowl until they are evenly distributed.

6. Pour and spread the filling evenly into the prepared dough in the pan. Bake at 180°C / 350°F for 30-40 minutes at the bottom of the oven, until the pastry has turned golden brown, and the filling has fully set and is no longer wobbly. Remove from the oven and let cool for about 10 minutes. Then, gently remove the tart from the pan and place on a wire rack. Whisk together icing ingredients and spread a thin layer on the tart while it's still a little warm.

   Optional: Garnish the tart with roughly chopped hazelnuts.

NEUCHÂTEL'S FAMOUS GROUND HAZELNUT TART

In Colombier, Switzerland, a special confiserie and tearoom with a mustard-yellow exterior sits across from the town hall. Across the front of the building, the Zurcher name appears in all capital letters. Operating at this location for more than 150 years, the most famous of all its sweet creations is the Gâteau aux noisettes ('hazelnut cake'). Made with ground hazelnuts and a short crust or puff pastry case, bakers here coat its surface with a thin layer of icing. The details of the recipe remain a secret, but this specialty now exists at bakeries and in private homes throughout the canton of Neuchâtel.

Théophile Zurcher opened his confiserie in 1862. Over the years, his establishment became known for its Gâteau aux amandes, an almond tart. In 1914, when the price increased around the time of World War I, the Zurcher bakery made this tart instead with ground hazelnuts. It became such a success that they never returned to using almonds.

Switzerland has another popular hazelnut tart in the canton of Bern. Known as the Haslikuchen, in reference to the Oberhasli region where it originated, you can also make it with a puff pastry or a short crust pastry. Instead of a powdered sugar glaze, like its counterpart in Neuchâtel, the surface of the Haslikuchen has a powdered sugar eagle made with a stencil. This symbol matches the coat of arms for the Oberhasli district. Moreover, the Haslikuchen has an optional layer of jam underneath the hazelnut filling, which I have incorporated into my recipe for the Gateau aux Noisettes.

The Gâteau aux noisettes is well known in the canton of Neuchâtel and comes in different sizes. Just like the Tarte aux pruneaux (Plum Tart, p. 143), one of my sons made this hazelnut tart in his elementary school classroom. I have talked with multiple people about mothers and grandmothers making it at home with their family recipes. The ingredients can vary, but the ground hazelnuts are always the star.

If you want to try the real thing, I recommend a visit to Zurcher's cozy, wood-paneled tearoom, still owned and operated by the same family. And if you can't make it to Colombier, I hope my recipe will give you a taste of this traditional sweet treat from the canton of Neuchâtel, where I have been living since 2012.

22 CARAC

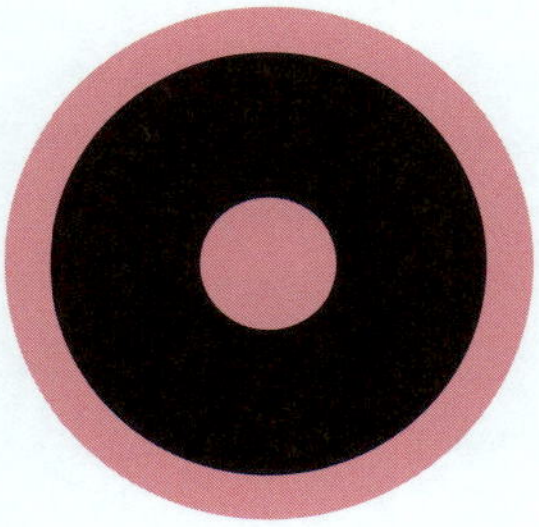

Preparation Time

approx. 5 hours

bake for 20 minutes

refrigerate for 2 hours

Quantity

Makes 8 little tarts.

Tools

Pastry rings or small tart pans with a diameter of about 7 ½-10 cm (3-4 inches)

INGREDIENTS

Pastry:

- 200 g (1 ½ cups + 1 tablespoon) all-purpose flour
- 50 g (¼ cup) sugar
- 25 g (5 tablespoons) ground hazelnuts or almonds
- ¼ teaspoon salt
- 85 g (6 tablespoons) unsalted butter, cold
- 1 egg, lightly beaten
- 1-2 tablespoons water, as needed

Chocolate ganache:

- 240 g (1 cup) heavy cream (35% milk fat)
- 250 g (8 ¾ ounces) dark chocolate, finely chopped
- 30 g unsalted butter (2 tablespoons), softened

Icing

- 80-100 g fresh spinach (3 ½ oz) (you won't use it all)
- 200 g (1 ¾ cups) powdered sugar
- 1-2 tablespoons water

INSTRUCTIONS

Pastry

1. Prepare the pastry dough. Whisk the flour, sugar, ground hazelnuts and salt together in a large bowl. Add the cold butter, in pieces, to the bowl. Using a pastry blender or two table knives, cut the butter into pieces, the size of small pebbles. Make a well in the center of the mixture and add the egg and 1-2 tablespoons of water, as needed. Stir together just until a dough forms. Form into a disk and wrap in parchment paper. Refrigerate the dough for 30-60 minutes.

2. When the dough is ready, grease pastry rings or tartelette pans (diameter: 7 ½-10 cm / 3-4 inches) with butter. Roll out the dough to a thickness of about 3 mm (about ¹⁄₁₀ of an inch) on a lightly floured surface with a rolling pin that has also been dusted lightly with flour. Cut out pieces of the dough to fit the pastry rings or pans, and gently place the dough in them (if you are using pastry rings, place them on

a baking sheet lined with parchment paper). Cut any excess dough from the sides and prick the bottom of the dough with a fork all over, to prevent air bubbles when it bakes.

Place them on a baking sheet lined with parchment paper and refrigerate the dough for 30 minutes.

3. Take the baking sheet with the chilled, prepared dough out of the fridge. Then, place pieces of parchment paper on top of the pastry rings or tart pans, then fill them up with dried beans or rice. Place the baking sheet with the dough back in the fridge to chill while you heat up the oven to 180° C / 350° F.

4. Once the oven is ready, blind bake the pastry dough for 15 minutes, and then remove parchment paper and dried beans or rice and bake for another 5-7 minutes until the dough becomes a light golden brown around the edges. Remove from the oven, cool for about 10 minutes, and then remove the pastry case from the pan and place on a wire rack to cool.

Chocolate ganache

5. Once the pastry shells have completely cooled, prepare the chocolate ganache filling. Add the heavy cream to a medium saucepan and bring it to a rolling boil. Take it off the heat immediately, and whisk in half of the finely chopped dark chocolate until it has completely melted and incorporated into the cream. Next, repeat the process with the remaining chocolate. Vigorously whisk in the butter until the mixture is thick and shiny—you can also use an immersion blender for this process. Pour the ganache into the baked pastry shells (leaving some room for the green icing) and refrigerate them for at least 2 hours.

Chocolate dots

6. While the ganache-filled pastry shells are cooling, use the leftover ganache to prepare the chocolate dot that gets placed on top of the green icing. Line a small baking sheet with some parchment paper. With a small spoon, take some of the ganache, and create a dot on the parchment paper. Repeat with the remaining ganache so you have at least eight nice dots. Refrigerate (or freeze) the chocolate dots, so they become firm.

Green icing

7. When the ganache-filled pastry shells and the chocolate dots have cooled, prepare the green icing. Wash the fresh spinach and steam it for several minutes in a small sauce pan filled partway with water and with a steamer basket. As soon as the spinach has wilted, rinse it with cold water and drain the excess liquid. Using an immersion or upright blender, puree the spinach into a fine paste.

8. Separately, in a medium-sized bowl, add the powdered sugar. Then, add in half a tablespoon of the pureed spinach. Carefully add more if you prefer a darker green color. Whisk it together with the powdered sugar, adding a tablespoon or two of water (as needed) to achieve a somewhat thick, but spreadable green icing. Please note: The amount of moisture from the spinach will determine how much additional water, if any, that you need to add to the icing. If your icing becomes too wet, just add some more powdered sugar to thicken it.

9. When you have achieved the ideal color and consistency for your green icing, add some to the center of a ganache-filled pastry shell and spread evenly and up to the edges of the tarts, so none of the ganache is exposed. Take

the chocolate dots out of the refrigerator, and gently place one on the center of your iced Carac, being careful not to touch the surface of the dot, as it will leave a fingerprint. Repeat this process with the remaining Carac. Place them back in the fridge to chill completely before serving. Or you can eat them right away if you can't wait.

Additional tips:

- You can use a Microplane grater to smooth out any rough edges of the baked pastry shells, after they have completely cooled.
- Instead of using water with the powdered sugar for the icing, you could use some egg white to make a green-tinted royal icing.

SWITZERLAND'S LITTLE GREEN TART WITH THE CHOCOLATE DOT

On an overcast day in June 2021, I arrived in Lausanne for the first-ever Caracathon. Organized by one of my favorite culinary associations in Switzerland, Lausanne à Table, this sold-out event allowed participants to visit up to 10 participating bakeries to pick up a Carac. While designed for people to visit these bakeries over the course of a month or so, I decided to truly fulfill the 'marathon' concept of the event by doing it all in one day. Overall, I managed to try a total of nine Caracs, missing just one. I still harbor some guilt over this, but I just ran out of time, energy and space in my stomach! I filled out my ballot online, ranking my favorites, and waited for the results. Over 400 people participated in the inaugural edition of this event.

Have you ever tried a Carac? This little tart has a chocolate ganache filling, a sweet pastry dough *(pâte sucrée)* and a distinct green icing. Historically, it has belonged to the professional sector. Caracs are less commonly made by people at home. As soon as I tried one, it became one of my absolute favorite Swiss desserts. However, with a very rich taste, they are not necessarily for everyone.

Caracs can appear at bakeries throughout Switzerland, sometimes as little bite-size *mignardises* (a sweet bite-sized dessert, typically served at the end of a meal), or even as full-sized tarts with servings the shape of thin triangular wedges. The way you usually see them, however, are as small individually portioned tarts, or *tartelettes*. While available throughout Switzerland, they have a particular connection to the canton of Vaud, where the Caracathon took place. Anecdotal evidence about the Carac in Suisse Romande, reported by Patrimoine Culinaire Suisse, indicates they date back to at least the 1920s.

Why the palindromic name? While we do not know for sure, the peculiar name of these tarts appears to have a connection to the origin of the chocolate used to first make them. For example, *cacao caraque* was the name given to a cocoa used by early chocolate makers in Switzerland, such as Philippe Suchard in the canton of Neuchâtel. *Caraques* is the French term for Caracas, Venezuela, for example. A 1958 manual for the *pâtisserie* ('pastry') sector published by Hans Kasper, a margarine producer at the time, includes a recipe for Tartelettes Caracas with green icing that looks like a modern-day Carac. Over the years, we can hypothesize that the name was shortened to the moniker we know today.

And why is the icing green? I wish I had the answer to this question! I did come across another manual for the confectionery sector that was published in Basel in the early 1950s and has a photo with a Carac-looking pastry. It was one of the pastries made for a Master Confectioners exam. The description indicates the pasty is baked empty, filled with ganache, iced with a pistachio fondant and topped with "un point chocolat." The black-and-white photo does not give proof whether the icing was green or not, but I think we can safely assume it was. Furthermore, it does not indicate whether the fondant was made with actual pistachios or with food coloring.

For my recipe, I add hazelnuts to the sweet pastry crust, keep the ganache really simple with just three ingredients and use pureed spinach to create a naturally green icing. Intended for home cooks, my recipe has relatively simple steps and not too many ingredients.

So, who won the first edition of the Caracathon? The Carac d'Or ('Golden Carac') went to Noz Chocolatier. I love a homemade Carac, but a professionally made Carac is also something special. With this new culinary competition, Lausanne is positioning itself to become the Swiss capital of the Carac. While it decidedly deserves this title, personally, one of my favorite Swiss Caracs comes from a bakery in the canton of Neuchâtel (if you ask me, I will tell you which one!).

23 SCHLORZIFLADEN

Preparation Time

approx. 1 hour 30 minutes

bake for 35-45 minutes

Quantity

Makes one tart.

8-10 servings

INGREDIENTS

Pear filling:

- 225 g (1 ¾ cups) whole dried pears, seeded, stemmed and quartered*
- 25 g (3 tablespoons) raisins
- 50 ml (¼ cup) kirsch
- 50 ml (¼ cup) orange juice
- 300 ml (1 ¼ cup) water
- 1 tablespoon sugar
- 1 teaspoon gingerbread spice

(recipe, see p. 80)

Dough:

- 225 g (1 ¾ cups) all-purpose flour
- 1 ½ tablespoons sugar
- ½ teaspoon salt
- 100 g (7 tablespoons) unsalted butter, cold
- 3-4 tablespoons water, cold

Cream topping:

- 3 eggs
- 300 ml (1 ¼ cups) heavy cream (35% milk fat)
- 100 ml (¼ cup + 3 tablespoons) milk
- 1 tablespoon all-purpose flour
- 2 tablespoons sugar
- 1 teaspoon vanilla extract or paste

*If you cannot find dried whole pears from Switzerland, you can substitute with sliced dried or dehydrated pears that still have a soft texture. However, please note that the color of the puree will not have the same dark-brown color.

INSTRUCTIONS

Pear filling

1. Place the pears in a medium-sized saucepan with all the remaining filling ingredients. Bring the mixture to a boil, and then let it simmer for about 45-60 minutes, until the fruit has softened. Let the mixture cool slightly, and then puree it until smooth with an immersion or upright blender. Refrigerate the mixture once it has cooled to room temperature.

   Please note: You can make the pear filling a day or two in advance and keep it refrigerated.

Pastry dough

2. Whisk together the flour, sugar and salt in a large bowl. Add the cold butter and use a pastry blender or a pair of table knives to cut it into pieces the size of small pebbles.

3. Make a well in the center of the mixture and add a few tablespoons of water. Stir together to form a dough, add extra water as necessary. Shape the dough into a disk, wrap it in parchment paper and refrigerate for 30-60 minutes.

4. When the dough has chilled, line a round tart pan (diameter: 28 cm, 11 inches) with parchment paper. Roll out the chilled dough and place it in the pan. Fit the dough into the pan. Prick the bottom of the dough with a fork. Spread the pear filling evenly over the dough in the pan. Return the tart to the refrigerator to chill.

Cream topping

5. Whisk the eggs together in a large bowl just until combined. Then, whisk in the remaining ingredients until well blended.

6. Take the prepared tart pan out of the fridge and pour the cream topping over the pear filling.

7. Bake the tart for 35-45 minutes at 180°C / 350°F at the bottom of the oven until the cream topping has set and browned slighted, and the pastry has also lightly browned. Let the tart cool in its pan for 10-15 minutes and then place it on a wire rack to cool. Serve with a dusting of powdered sugar or some whipped cream.

A SLICE OF SCHLORZIFLADEN WITH MOUNTAIN VIEWS

Also known as a Doppelfladen ('double fladen'), the Schlorzifladen has two layers: a dried pear puree and a cream topping. The region where you will find it uses the suffix *-fladen* to describe round, flat cakes, such as the Zimtfladen (p. 111) and the round gingerbread known as Biberfladen. The term *schlorzi* describes the bottom layer of the tart, a dark brown filling made from *dörrbirnen* (dried pears). Countless variations exist for this tart, made by bakeries, restaurants and home cooks. I associate it with alpine views, because the first two times I had it were both at mountain restaurants in Eastern Switzerland.

My introduction to this tart was at the famous Berggasthaus Äscher, nestled into the cliffs of the Alpstein mountains. This incredible location has received a lot of attention in recent years after being featured on the cover of National Geographic's *Destinations of a Lifetime* in 2015. Located in the Swiss canton of Appenzell Innerrhoden, my family and I visited this restaurant and guesthouse early in the morning. We successfully arrived before the onslaught of eager tourists hoping to snap a photo of this highly Instagrammable landmark.

We grabbed one of the few remaining open tables outside, some of which already had signs declaring them as reserved. After placing our order, the waitress brought me an oval plate with a large rectangular slice and a row of whipped cream piped along its side. This version of the tart had a light, creamy topping with a thin layer of dried pear filling underneath. Its surface had a golden to dark-brown patina. With some hot coffee and a spectacular view, this was a wonderful way to first experience this tart.

My second taste of the Schlorzifladen took place at the summit of Mount Säntis. At 2,502 meters (8,209 feet), this mountain has the highest peak in the Alpstein massif. It falls within three Swiss cantons: Appenzell Ausserrhoden, Appenzell Innerrhoden and St. Gallen. From the summit of Mount Säntis, you can catch a glimpse of no less than six countries on a clear day: France, Germany, Italy, Austria, Liechtenstein and Switzerland.

At the Säntisgipfel restaurant, the Schlorzifladen had a more yellow-hued cream layer, similar to a thick custard. The triangular slice came from a round tart, the more traditional shape for this dessert. Its surface was lightly browned in the oven, in comparison to the one from the Äscher. The restaurant served it with a scoop of walnut ice cream, and like the first one I tried, a generous amount of whipped cream, which seems to be a standard accompaniment.

Of course, you can buy the pear filling premade, but there comes a certain satisfaction when you make it yourself. Swiss dried pears are a special product, because unlike any dried pears I had in the United States, producers dry these pears whole. This process, carried on for centuries, makes them soft, shriveled and dark brown. They have a sweet, almost caramelized pear flavor. Depending on the producer, they can also be quite moist inside. Along with the Schlorzifladen, I like using them for breads, like the Bündner Birnbrot or the Luzerner Birnenweggen. You can also find them in a traditional dessert from the canton of Uri called Brischtner Nytlä. The pears are cooked in red wine and served with lots of whipped cream.

One early summer day, when I visited Chef Carlos Alexander Navarro at Restaurant Rechberg in Zürich to talk about Swiss desserts, he told me that the Schlorzifladen was one of his favorites. Swiss culinary journalist Sarah Kohler also brought up this tart when I asked her about sweet dishes from Switzerland during a press event in Pontresina. Their recommendations, and my mountain restaurant experiences, are the reasons I chose to include this dried pear tart in this book.

I never had anything like the Schlorzifladen until I moved to Switzerland, and it has become one of my (many) favorites. Whenever I say its name, it reminds me of the sing-song quality of the Swiss German language. My homemade version will hopefully give you a taste of this alpine specialty, but you will also have to seek it out yourself when you visit the two half-cantons of Appenzell or the Toggenburg region of St. Gallen.

24 SOLOTHURNERLI

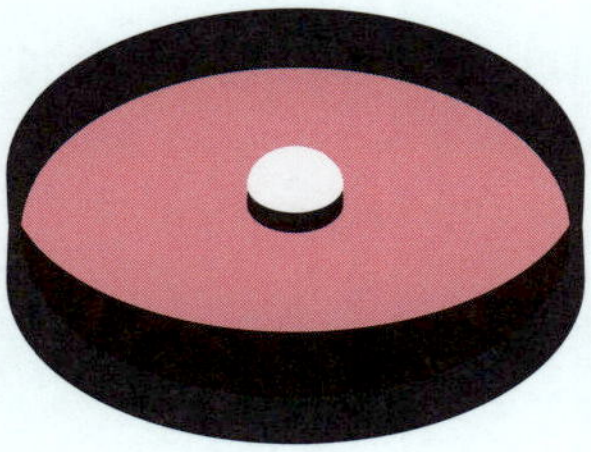

Preparation Time
approx. 3-4 hours
bake for 2 hours 30 minutes

Quantity
Makes 6 cakes.

Tools
Pastry rings with a diameter of about 8.25 cm (3 ¼ inches) and a piping bag

INGREDIENTS

Hazelnut meringue (Japonais):

- 150 g (¾ cup) sugar
- 1 tablespoon cornstarch
- 3 egg whites (about 120 g)
- a pinch of salt
- 30 g (6 tablespoons) ground hazelnuts

Hazelnut sponge cake:

- 40 g (3 tablespoons) unsalted butter
- 40 g (3 tablespoons) sugar
- 1 egg yolk
- 100 g (¾ cup) all-purpose flour
- 50 g (⅔ cup) ground hazelnuts
- ½ teaspoon baking powder
- 125 ml (½ cup) milk
- 1 egg white

Buttercream frosting:

- 225 g (2 cups) powdered sugar
- 115 g (½ cup) unsalted butter, softened
- 1-2 tablespoons milk
- ½ teaspoon vanilla

To decorate the cake:

- 40-50 g (½ to ⅔ cup) ground hazelnuts
- 6 whole hazelnuts

INSTRUCTIONS

Hazelnut meringue (Japonais)

1. Make the hazelnut meringue layers. Line a baking sheet with parchment paper. Use a pencil to draw 12 circles that match the diameter of the pastry rings you are using, about 8 ¼ cm (3 ¼ inches). Flip the pieces of parchment paper over, so the side that you've written on is touching the bottom of the baking sheet.

2. Prepare the hazelnut meringue. Whisk together the sugar and cornstarch. Set aside. Use an electric mixer with a balloon whisk attachment and beat the egg whites together with a pinch of salt, until they become fluffy and form stiff peaks.

3. Continue to whisk the egg whites with the electric mixer, adding in a tablespoon of the sugar and cornstarch mixture from time to time, for a period of about four minutes, until the mixture becomes thick and shiny.

4. Fold in the ground hazelnuts until well combined, being careful not to knock out all the air from the mixture. Add it to a piping bag with a small round opening. Start in the center of the circle and spiral the mixture to create a circle (approx. 5-6 cm / 1/4 inch tall) that matches the shape of the pencil circles you've drawn on the parchment paper.

5. Place the tray of 12 hazelnut meringues in an oven preheated to 90°C / 195°F. Carefully, using a wooden spoon, prop the oven door open, so steam can escape from the meringues as they dry out. Keep them in the oven at this temperature for about 1 1/2 hours.

6. When the meringues have fully dried out, peel away the parchment paper and place them on a wire rack. While they are cooling, you can start making the hazelnut cakes.

Hazelnut cakes

7. Grease 6 pastry rings (diameter: 8 ¼ cm or 3 ¼ inches) with butter, and place them on a baking sheet lined with parchment paper. Set aside.

8. In a large bowl, stir together the butter and sugar until the mixture becomes creamy and well combined. Stir in the egg yolk until the mixture is smooth. Set aside.

9. In a separate bowl, whisk together the flour, ground hazelnuts and baking powder. In two batches, add the flour mixture and milk to the mixture in the large bowl, stirring just until the ingredients are well incorporated.

10. Add the egg white to a bowl with a pinch of sugar, and then whisk it by hand or with an electric mixer until it forms stiff peaks. Carefully fold the egg white into the cake batter until it's evenly distributed.

11. Spoon the cake batter into the prepared pastry rings, so the batter is equally distributed. Bake them for about 15 minutes at 180°C / 350°F, until a toothpick inserted into their center comes out clean.

12. Let them cool on the baking sheet for about 10 minutes, and then carefully remove the cake from the rings. Place the little cakes on a wire rack to cool.

Frosting

13. When the cakes have fully cooled, prepare the frosting. Sift the powdered sugar into a bowl. Add the remaining ingredients and combine them by hand, or with an electric mixer, until you have a smooth, creamy and spreadable frosting. If the frosting is too wet, you can add some more powdered sugar. If it's too thick, you can add a little water.

Assemble the cakes

14. To assemble the cakes, first frost the top of one hazelnut meringue. Next, spread a layer of frosting on top of a hazelnut cake and stack it on top of the frosted hazelnut meringue. After that, add a another hazelnut meringue on top of the frosted hazelnut cake. Then, spread a thin layer of frosting evenly on the sides of the cake. Press the ground hazelnuts against the sides of the cake so they stick. Finally, add a little dot of frosting on the top of the cake in the middle and attach one hazelnut to it. Repeat this with the remaining 5 cakes. Refrigerate the cakes before serving.

SOLOTHURN'S FANCY HAZELNUT LAYER CAKE

The baroque town of Solothurn has a special layered cake with a history that stretches back over 100 years. Albert Studer is credited with inventing the Solothurner Torte at his bakery there. While this establishment has since changed hands several times over the years, the cake has remained, with slight adjustments along the way. In all, this cake has five sweet layers. It represents a category of fine cakes in Switzerland connected to particular geographic areas, such as the Zuger Kirschtorte and the Engadiner Torte.

At the Suteria bakery in Solothurn, you can find about five different sizes of the Solothurner Torte, made with the Studer's original recipe. The cakes are a sandwich of two hazelnut meringues, known as Japonais, with a hazelnut sponge cake in the middle. A light hazelnut icing surrounds all these various layers, and shaved toasted hazelnuts are pressed into the sides of the cake. At least two other bakeries in town offer their own versions of this cake as well: Kaffeehalle Solothurn and Confiserie Hofer.

You may be wondering why the Solothurner Torte has a layer named "Japonais". The hazelnut meringue layer in the Zuger Kirschtorte also carries this name. One theory connects it to a nickname for a popular Swiss cookie, often referred to as Japonais. Sherly, of Sherly's Kitchen in Zürich, used to work for an engineering company in Switzerland that produced industrial machines for cookie manufacturers. She told me where she learned about the origin of this name. When she asked the head engineer at the company about the origin of the name for the company's hazelnut meringue cookies, he told Sherly that "of course, nowadays all these cookies are industrialized so we produce a flat-shaped Japonais cookie or cake bottom. But before these cookies were industrialized, the old Japonais cookies used to be hand-piped. When they were hand-piped, the cookies had a small peak making them look like a traditional Japanese hat. That's why they were called "Japonais." So, it seems the *kasa*, a traditional woven hat from Japan, could be the inspiration for the name.

For making the Solothurner Torte at home, I chose to create a recipe for the smallest version of this cake, the Solothurnerli. These festive homemade cakes take some time, but they are perfect for celebrations with family and friends.

25 TARTE À LA RAISINÉE

From Romano Hasenauer, Auberge du Chalet-des-Enfants in Le Mont-sur-Lausanne (Vaud)

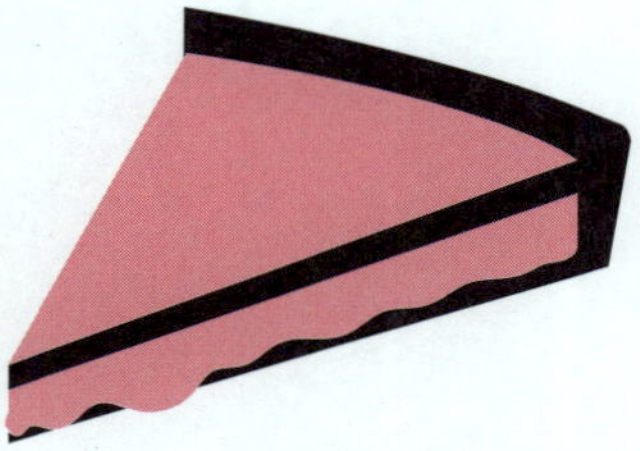

Preparation Time
approx. 1 hour 30 minutes
bake for approx. 1 hour 20 minutes

Quantity
Makes one tart.
10-12 servings

INGREDIENTS

Pastry:

- 130 g (½ cup + 2 tablespoons) unsalted butter, cold
- 250 g (2 cups) all-purpose flour
- 6 g (1 teaspoon) salt
- 100 ml (⅓ cup + 2 tablespoons) water, cold

Filling:

- 5 eggs**
- 200 g (1 cup) sugar
- 200 g (½ cup + 3 tablespoons) *raisinée**
- 200 g (¾ cup + 2 tablespoons) heavy cream (35% milk fat)
- 100 g (scant ½ cup) milk

*In Switzerland, you can substitute *raisinée* with *vin cuit* or *cougnarde*. In the United States, you can purchase or make boiled apple or pear cider, which can be substituted for these ingredients.

**For this recipe, you should use medium-sized eggs (53 g / 1.9 oz). In the US, these would typically be considered large eggs.

INSTRUCTIONS

1. Make the pastry dough. Using your fingers, break up the butter with the flour and salt until it becomes fully incorporated and evenly distributed within the mixture.

2. Add the water and incorporate it completely, kneading as little as possible. Add a little extra water or flour, if necessary, to form the dough.

3. Let the dough rest for one hour in the refrigerator before using.

4. Roll out the dough and place it in a round tart pan with a diameter of about 32 cm (12 ½ inches), lined with parchment paper.

5. Cover the dough with another sheet of parchment paper and cover with dry beans (about 1 kg).

6. Bake the dough for 40 minutes in an oven preheated to 165°C / 325°F. Just before the last 5 minutes of baking, take the baking sheet out of the oven. Remove the dried beans (which

can be used again for the same purpose). Put the pan back in the oven and let the pastry bake for another 5 minutes or so, just until it becomes golden.

7. Mix the eggs, but without whipping them, to avoid foaming. Add the other ingredients, mix well and pour them through a sieve over the precooked dough.

8. Bake for 40-50 minutes at 95°C / 200°F in a convection oven or at 110°C / 225°F in a conventional oven (top / bottom heat), just until the filling sets. Let it cool completely before cutting.

A SWEET BROWN TART IN THE FOREST ABOVE LAUSANNE

In the hills above Lausanne, nestled within the Jorat forest, sits the historic Auberge du Chalet-des-Enfants. This cozy restaurant takes its name from the Secrétan family that lived at this location during the 18th century. Formerly known as the 'Chalet aux enfants à Secrétan,' the name shortened over the years to its current form.

The legend goes that fashion designer Coco Chanel, who lived in Lausanne at the Beau-Rivage Palace from 1945 to 1954, used to take her walks in this bucolic setting. During these peaceful promenades, she would stop from time to time at the restaurant for milk and a flan dessert.

Decades later, I sat on the terrace with my family, overlooking the vegetable gardens at the restaurant. Instead of flan, no longer on the menu, I ordered a slice of the famous Vaudois specialty, Tarte à la raisinée. The texture of this tart's shiny brown filling almost resembles a flan. I should tell you that I was not such a fan of this tart when I first tried it years earlier. Over time, however, it has become one of my favorites. It has a unique, rich caramelized flavor and a very sweet taste.

With a word like *raisinée* in its name, you could certainly imagine a tart with raisins in it (*raisin* means 'grapes' in French), like the Goms Tätere from Valais. Or, you might think it contains wine, like the Gâteau au vin ('wine cake'), also from Vaud. Instead, you make this tart with a thick, dark and super-sweet syrup typically made from apple juice, pear juice or a mixture of the two. The Auberge du Chalet-des-Enfants uses a *raisinée* cooked over a wood fire that has a beautiful color when mixed with cream and baked in a pastry shell. Patrimoine Culinaire Suisse has found evidence of something known as *raisinée* from the 17th century in Switzerland. This early version, however, describes a thick jam made with apples and pears, cooked in a concentrated grape juice. Other examples also describe the use of grapes, but over the centuries, they no longer appear as an ingredient in this product. The name, however, has been carried on.

You will find a similar product in the canton of Fribourg called *vin cuit* (literally translated, it means 'cooked wine'), which I often see made with 100% pear juice, but it can also contain apple juice. People use it to make a similar tart in Fribourg, popular during the autumn feast known as Bénichon, aptly known as the Tarte au vin cuit.

When sugar was scarce, during a period of time up until the end of World War II, boiling down apple and pear juice into a thick syrup provided another form of more affordable sweetness that could be preserved during the winter months. While similar to *Birnel* or *Birnendicksaft*, a pear syrup made in central Switzerland with clarified pear juice (which I use as an ingredient in my Lebkuchen recipe, p. 79), *raisinée* contains unfiltered juice.

Romano Hasenauer, proprietor of the Auberge du Chalet-des-Enfants, did not start making Tarte à la raisinée until he took over the restaurant in 2005. The restaurant offers sweet dishes from the canton, like its famous tart, and other classic dishes from Switzerland with local ingredients such as meringues with double cream from the farm next door. Starting in 2016, they have built up their gardens around the property, supplying ingredients for their kitchen. It also has a small on-your-honor shop where you can buy a bottle of the same *raisinée* they use for their famous tart.

Thinking back on the first time I went to the Auberge du Chalet-des-Enfants, it was as a jury member for the Boutefas sausage contest (another Vaudois specialty). I ate a copious amount of pork sausage that night—not quite comparable to the glamourous coffee break of Ms. Chanel. My second visit to the restaurant, with a slice of the Tarte à la raisinée and its flan-like filling, followed by a walk in the forest, thankfully came closer to the legendary visits by the French fashion designer. Whether you make this tart at home or order it at the restaurant, it is one of those Swiss desserts and a culinary tradition in Vaud that you really must try in your lifetime.

AUBERGE DU CHALET-DES-ENFANTS

Rte du Chalet-des-Enfants
1052 Le Mont-sur-Lausanne
+41 (0) 21 784 44 80
auberge@chaletdesenfants.ch
chaletdesenfants.ch

26 TARTE AUX PRUNEAUX

Preparation Time
approx. 1 hour 30 minutes
bake for 35-40 minutes

Quantity
Makes one tart.
6-8 servings

INGREDIENTS

Dough:

- 225 g (1 ¾ cups) all-purpose flour
- ¼ teaspoon salt
- zest of one organic lemon
- 100 g (7 tablespoons) unsalted butter, cold
- 1 egg
- 1-2 tablespoons water, cold

Filling:

- 50 g (about ½ cup) leftover cookies, finely crushed/crumbled*
- about 1 ⅕ kg plums (about 2 ⅔ lb)
- 1-2 tablespoons sugar

Brush on after baking (optional):

- 1-2 tablespoons honey, gently warmed

*Any type of stale cookie that can be easily crushed into fine crumbs works for this recipe. For example, you could use leftover Grassins (p. 165) or Zimtstängel (p. 181) for this purpose.

INSTRUCTIONS

1. Make the dough. Whisk together the flour, salt and lemon zest in a large bowl. Add the cold butter and use a pastry blender or a pair of table knives to cut the butter into pieces the size of small pebbles.

2. Make a well in the center of the mixture and add the egg and 1-2 tablespoons of cold water. Stir everything together to form a dough. Shape the dough into a disk, wrap it in parchment paper and refrigerate it for 30-60 minutes.

3. When the dough has chilled, line a round tart pan (diameter: 28 cm, 11 inches) with parchment paper or grease a non-stick pan with butter. Roll out the chilled dough on the sheet of parchment paper to fit the diameter of the pan. Invert the sheet of parchment paper onto the prepared pan and peel off the paper. Fit the dough into the pan. Prick the bottom of the dough with a fork. Spread crushed cookies evenly over the bottom of the pastry.

4. Next, gently arrange the pitted and quartered plums on top of the crushed cookies. You can pack the plums tightly and overlap them a bit as they will shrink somewhat as they bake. Then, sprinkle sugar over the fresh plums.

5. Bake for about 35-40 minutes at 200°C / 400°F, until the plums have softened and the crust is lightly browned. Optional: If you would like to make the tart shine a bit more and add an additional bit of sweetness, you can gently warm a couple tablespoons of honey and brush them on the baked plums while the tart is still warm.

A SEASONAL PLUM TART TO BREAK A FAST

I credit my knowledge of local food traditions in the canton of Neuchâtel, in part, to the experiences of my boys in their public school classrooms. My second year in Switzerland, my then 5-year-old son came home with a little plum tart he had made at school, wrapped in a paper napkin. This little tart introduced me to the local holiday known as Jeûne fédéral ('Federal Fast').

The majority of French-speaking cantons of Switzerland eat Tarte aux pruneaux (plum tart) this time of year, not only because these plums are in season, but also because of a regional holiday. Historically, fasting days in Switzerland date back centuries, as a moral and spiritual tradition for seeking penance. Cantons of both Protestant and Catholic affiliations in Switzerland committed this sacrifice in times of war, illness, famine or as a way to give thanks. A traditional fast-breaking dish was the Tarte aux pruneaux. It could be made in advance, if people were spending the day listening to sermons in church, for example.

No longer a day of fasting, Jeûne fédéral has become a good excuse to bake a plum tart. The cantons of Vaud and Geneva recognize a fasting day in September as well. In Neuchâtel and Vaud, the Monday after the Jeûne fédéral (Lundi de jeûne) is a day off from school and work for much of the canton. In comparison, Geneva celebrates Jeûne genevois on the Thursday following the first Sunday in September.

Some recipes for Tarte aux pruneaux add a *guélon*, also referred to as a *liaison*. This generally refers to a mixture of egg with cream or milk that gets poured over the plums before baking. It creates a custard-like filling to accompany the fruit. I prefer this plum tart *sans guélon* in order to maximize the flavor of the fruit.

For me, this Swiss plum tart holiday helps usher in the change of seasons, with the approaching arrival of cooler temperatures and the beginning of autumn. It also helps mark the years, reminding me of a time when my sweet little son was so proud to show me his handmade Tarte aux pruneaux after school.

V

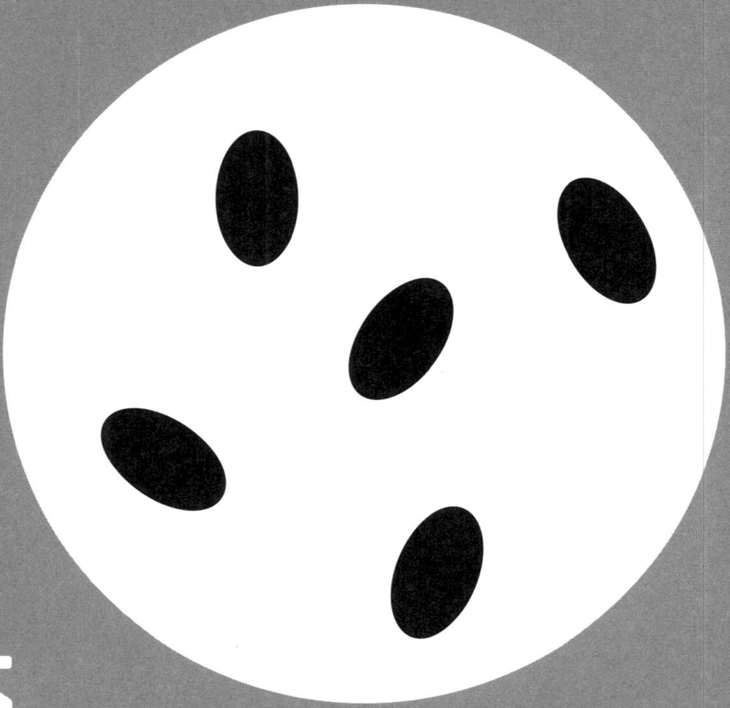

COOKIES
GUETZLI
BISCUITS

V. COOKIES

My goal for this chapter is to present recipes for some cookies well-known throughout Switzerland, in addition to several lesser-known, regional recipes. Most importantly though, you should know that this country takes its cookie-baking seriously. The Swiss German language even has a special word specifically to describe the act of making cookies at Christmas: *guezle*. Three of the most popular Christmas cookies in Switzerland all require cookie cutters: Mailänderli (lemon shortbread cookies), Basler Brunsli (spiced chocolate cookies) or Zimtsterne (cinnamon stars). You will find recipes for these three cookies via my blog.

While these three Christmas cookies have national recognition, many only exist in their canton of origin, such as the Drusenzelte in Glarus (p. 161) or Grassins in Graubünden (p. 165). Oftentimes, these cookies have connections to local traditions, such as the Seisler Brätzele (p. 169) in Fribourg for *chilbi* celebrations in the autumn or Crèfli in Ticino during the Christmas and New Year's holiday season.

Cookies have a certain versatility, appearing throughout the day for a snack or dessert—and even for the first meal of the day. In Ticino, when I stayed overnight at a bed and breakfast on a berry farm near the Italian border, the breakfast buffet included little chocolate and vanilla shortbread cookies. More of an Italian tradition, this practice is certainly less common in Switzerland's other linguistic regions. Cookies for breakfast always seem like a good idea though, in my opinion.

The recipes I have chosen for this book include a few examples of what might be considered Switzerland's 'national cookies,' such as Spitzbuben (although with different names in different regions). With dozens and perhaps even hundreds of Swiss cookies, this chapter gives only a sample of some classics and some regional specialties, but there are so many more to discover and enjoy!

22 BASLER LECKERLI

Preparation Time

at least 1 hour 30 minutes

bake for 10-15 minutes

Quantity

Makes approx. 45 biscuits.

INGREDIENTS

- 175 g (1 ⅓ cups + 1 tablespoon) all-purpose flour
- 150 g (1 ¼ cups) whole wheat flour
- 1 teaspoon ground cinnamon
- ¾ teaspoon baking soda
- ¼ teaspoon ground cloves
- ¼ teaspoon ground nutmeg
- ¼ teaspoon salt
- 105 g (5 tablespoons) honey
- 75 g (⅓ cup) sugar
- 100 ml (¼ cup + 3 tablespoons) orange juice
- 1 tablespoon kirsch
- zest of one organic lemon
- 100 g (¾ cup + 2 tablespoons) slivered almonds
- 50 g (¼ cup) candied orange peel, finely chopped
- 46 g (¼ cup) candied ginger, finely chopped*

Brush on top:

- 80 g (½ + 3 tablespoons cups) powdered sugar
- 1-2 tablespoons water
- 1 teaspoon lemon juice (or kirsch)

*If you don't like candied ginger, feel free to increase the amount of candied orange peel to 100 grams.

INSTRUCTIONS

1. In a large bowl, whisk together the following ingredients: all-purpose flour, wheat flour, cinnamon, baking soda, cloves, nutmeg and salt. Make a well in the center of the mixture and set aside.

2. Separately, in a heat-safe bowl, gently whisk the honey and sugar together over a water bath (bain-marie). Carefully remove the bowl from the heat when the honey has softened and the sugar is completely incorporated into the honey. Next, whisk in the orange juice, kirsch and lemon zest. Stir together with the flour mixture, just until a dough starts to form. Then, add the remaining ingredients: almonds, candied orange peel and candied ginger. Stir until they are evenly distributed in the dough.

3. Roll out the dough onto a sheet of parchment paper lightly dusted with flour. You can also lightly dust the rolling pin with flour to prevent the dough from sticking. Form the dough into

1-2 large rectangles, about 3 mm thick (about 1⁄10 inch). Cover the dough and refrigerate it for about an hour or overnight.

4. Place the dough on a baking sheet lined with parchment paper. Bake at 200°C / 400°F for about 10-15 minutes until the surface becomes a light golden brown.

5. Let the baked sheet of Leckerli cool for several minutes while you prepare the glaze. Whisk together the powdered sugar with the water and lemon juice or kirsch and brush it on the warm Leckerli. Next, using a sharp knife, press down firmly on the dough to cut it into pieces about 3 x 4 cm (about 1 ¼ x 1 ½ inches). Place them on a wire rack to fully cool. Store them in an airtight container.

CHEWY, RECTANGULAR GINGERBREAD BISCUITS FROM BASEL

"Your leckerli are on point! Absolutely delicious... I remember my father making some back in Canada... ended up in an argument because the dough was so thick he killed the mixer's motor and my mom got real pissed lol."

This message showed up in my inbox, and I smiled when I read it. I had heard about Leckerli dough being really thick and hard to work with. To my recipe, I add a lot of orange juice, so my electric mixer doesn't have to work as hard to form the dough. These cookies from Basel are one of my favorites, and I had never tasted anything like them until I moved to Switzerland.

You should also note that people use lots of different, but similar names for these rectangular biscuits. In addition to Leckerli, you'll find them referred to as Läckerli, Leckerly and Läggerli. Some may describe this gingerbread as tough, but I prefer to think of them as chewy. They used to be reserved just for the holiday season, but now you see them all the time and not just in Basel. My local supermarket in French-speaking Switzerland sells bags of Leckerli year-round, for example.

In terms of the history of Leckerli, the earliest evidence of this biscuit in Switzerland comes from the 17th century, according to research conducted by author Albert Spycher-Gautschi. Others have claimed it stretches back to the 15th century, as an invention of the Council of Basel. Over the years, Basel became the epicenter for this special biscuit. It has a long history in the canton, reaching back centuries. The oldest Leckerli company in the city, Jakob's Basler Läckerli, started in 1753.

Those of you who really know these biscuits will see that I have made some non-traditional changes to my recipe with the addition of whole wheat flour and candied ginger. Store them in a sealed container and they last for a few weeks. They are especially nice as a homemade gift during the holiday season or to keep around for impromptu guests.

28 CIAMBELLE

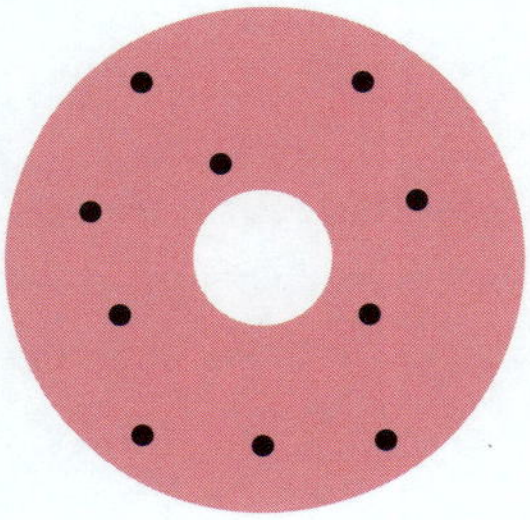

Preparation Time

approx. 1 hour 30 minutes
bake for 12-15 minutes

Quantity

Makes approx. 48 cookies.

INGREDIENTS

Dry ingredients:

- 350 g (2 ¾ cups) all-purpose flour
- 7 g (1 tablespoon) anise seeds
- 7 g (1 tablespoon) caraway seeds
- ¾ teaspoon baking soda
- ¼ teaspoon salt

Wet ingredients:

- 75 g (⅓ cup) unsalted butter, softened
- 150 g (¾ cup) sugar
- 2 eggs
- 2 tablespoons milk
- 1 teaspoon vanilla extract or paste

INSTRUCTIONS

1. In a large bowl, whisk together the dry ingredients. Set aside.

2. In another large bowl, cream together the butter and sugar until well combined. Then add the eggs, milk and vanilla to the bowl and mix until these ingredients are fully incorporated and the mixture has a smooth texture.

3. Add the dry ingredients to the large bowl with the wet ingredients and stir together until a dough forms. Refrigerate the dough for about 30-60 minutes.

4. Once the dough has chilled, make it into cylinders with a width of about 1 ¼ cm (½ inch) and about 7 ½ cm (3-4 inches) long. Bring the end of the cylinder together to form a cookie wreath. Place on a baking sheet lined with parchment paper. Repeat this process until all the dough is used.

5. Bake the cookies for approximately 12-15 minutes at 180°C / 350°F, until they become a light golden brown. Let them cool on the baking sheet for a few minutes, and then place them on wire racks to cool. Store the cookies in an airtight container.

FRAGRANT DOUGHNUT-SHAPED COOKIES FROM TICINO

The word *ciambelle* in Italian means 'doughnut' or 'ring-shaped object.' In Switzerland, it also refers to a crumbly ring-shaped cookie found in the Italian-speaking canton of Ticino. Made with a combination of anise and caraway seeds, these biscuits have a lovely fragrance and taste.

In Switzerland, Lugano is considered somewhat of the birthplace of these cookies. They have historically been popular in taverns, available in glass jars on the counter for those who want one with a glass of red wine or to dip in their coffee. I met someone who remembers making them in school in Ticino when she was a kid. Recipes get passed down from generation to generation.

Former opera singer and food blogger David Anchel in New York City tested my recipe for me, after which he wrote, "I must say I really love these cookies. They are perfect with coffee or just a wonderful way to end a meal."

The Italian saying *non tutte le ciambelle riescono col buco* ('not all doughnuts turn out with a hole') is apparently used to try and make people feel better when they experience a failure or things don't go as planned. A similar saying about staying positive when facing adversity comes from a song by Burl Ives in the United States, "As you go through life make this your goal, watch the donut, not the hole." Perhaps, if you know someone going through a tough time, you might want to bake a batch of these cookies for them, place them in a glass jar and write a note for them with one of these expressions.

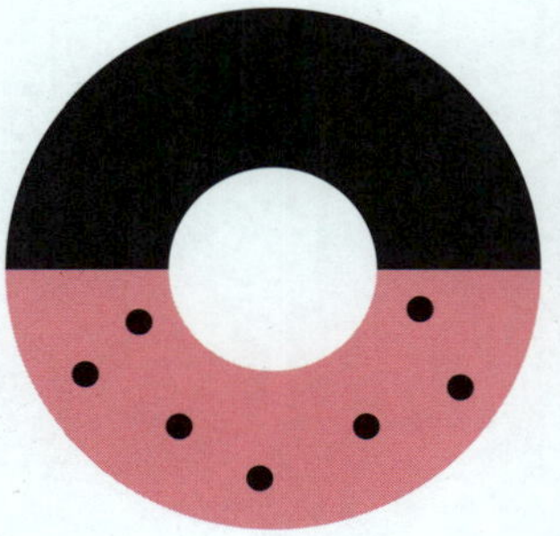

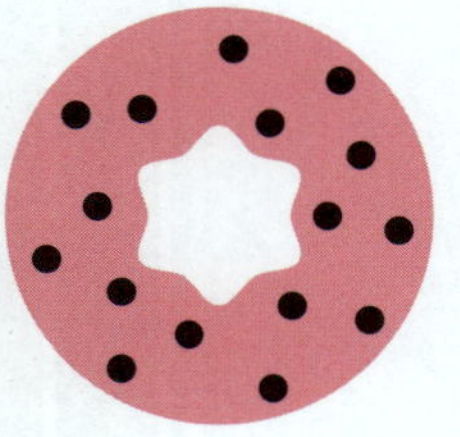

NORDIC WARE

29 CRÈFLI

Preparation Time
approx. 1 hour 15 minutes
bake for 10-12 minutes

Quantity
Makes approx. 15-18 cookies.

INGREDIENTS

- 300 g (2 ⅓ cups + 1 tablespoon) all-purpose flour
- 1 teaspoon baking powder
- ½ teaspoon salt
- ¼ teaspoon nutmeg
- 100 g (½ cup) sugar
- 75 g (3 ½ tablespoons) honey
- 50 g (3 ½ tablespoons) unsalted butter
- 50 ml (scant ¼ cup) milk
- 1 tablespoon nocino (or grappa)
- 1 teaspoon vanilla extract or paste

INSTRUCTIONS

1. In a large bowl, whisk together the dry ingredients: all-purpose flour, baking powder, nutmeg and salt. Make a well in the center of the mixture. Set aside.

2. In a medium saucepan, add the sugar, honey and butter. Whisk the mixture together over low heat until the sugar has completely dissolved. When it has a smooth texture, stir in the milk, nocino (or grappa) and vanilla until well combined.

3. Pour the gently warmed wet ingredients into the center of the large bowl with the dry ingredients. Stir together until it creates a dough.

4. On a lightly floured surface, roll out the dough so it's about 3 mm thick (about ⅒ inch). Use a cookie press to make an impression in the dough, if you wish. Then, cut them out into circles or rectangles (their traditional shape). Place them on a baking sheet lined with parchment paper. Next, put them in the fridge to chill for about 15-30 minutes.

5. Bake them for about 8-10 minutes at 200°C / 400°F. When the surface of the cookies has lightly browned, remove them from the oven, let them rest for a few minutes on the baking sheet, and then place them on a wire rack to cool completely.

FORTIFYING HONEY COOKIES FROM ALTA LEVENTINA

Colorful frescoes adorn the exterior of the Casa Stanga, built in the 16th century in Giornico (Ticino). They depict over 50 coats of arms of travelers who stayed at this former inn. Since 1972, it has housed the Museo di Leventina. Part of the museum's collection includes a heart-shaped mold, carved out of wood, used for making Crèfli. These honey cookies have a long history in this picturesque valley.

Located southeast of the Gotthard Pass, Giornico was an important connection point for people traveling along this major trade and transportation route. It has a dramatic natural landscape, surrounded by vineyards and nestled in the mountainous Leventina Valley. No longer bustling with travelers, Giornico has reminders of its past, such as the Casa Stanga. The museum there provides a glimpse into the history of this valley and is well worth a visit during your time in this small town.

Typically made in a rectangular shape, Crèfli have a firm texture. Bakers press the dough into a mold, leaving a decorative motif on its surface. It's said that in the past, mail carriers used to enjoy these cookies because they provided sustenance during their travel over the mountain pass. Those responsible with shoveling snow along the route are also said to have enjoyed these cookies. Today, you can find Crèfli throughout the year, but they are also traditionally given as gifts around the holiday season, and for some, on the first day of the new year. Another related cookie from this area is the Spampezie, also often made with a motif pressed into its surface and with a spiced ground nut filling. Like the Spampezie, a version of Crèfli from Giornico also contains a filling.

I wish I could talk with the person who carved this beautiful wooden mold at the museum. Did someone carve it for their sweetheart? Were the Crèfli used for a special occasion, such as a wedding? Or were the cookies made and shipped to someone to help them remember the village that they left?

Crèfli mold, as exhibited at the Museo di Leventina

My questions remain unanswered, but back at home, I love making Crèfli. Instead of heart-shaped molds, I use aluminum cookie stamps in my own kitchen. To the recipe, I add a splash of nocino, a green walnut liqueur from Ticino. In some ways, the flavor of these cookies reminds me of an American graham cracker, but with a tradition that remains entirely Swiss.

30 DRUSENZELTE

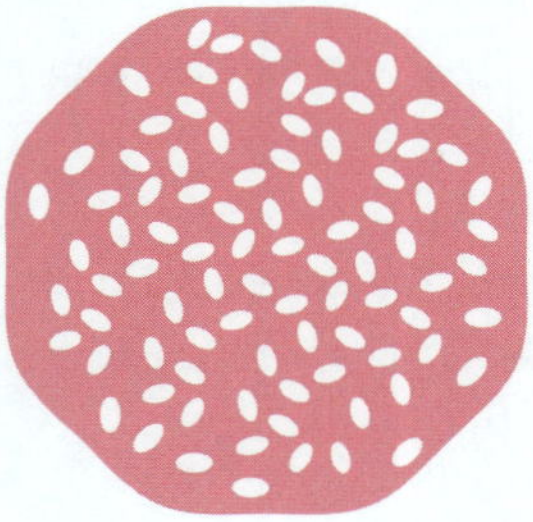

Preparation Time
approx. 45 minutes
bake for 12-15 minutes

Quantity
Makes 3 large cookies.

INGREDIENTS

- 250 g (2 cups) all-purpose flour
- 1 teaspoon baking powder
- ¼ teaspoon salt
- 170 g (¾ cup) unsalted butter, softened
- 75 g (⅓ cup) sugar
- 2 eggs
- 50 g (⅓ cup) raisins

Before baking:

- 1 egg, beaten
- pearl sugar (or granulated sugar)

INSTRUCTIONS

1. Heat the oven to 200˚C / 400˚F.

2. Add the flour, baking powder and salt to a bowl and whisk together until well combined. Set aside.

3. In a large bowl or with an electric mixer, cream together the butter and sugar. Next, stir in the two eggs, one at a time, until completely incorporated into the mixture.

4. Add the flour mixture to the large bowl with the wet ingredients. Stir just until the flour is incorporated and then mix in the raisins until they are evenly distributed.

5. If the dough is too soft, you can place it in the refrigerator for about 10-15 minutes to cool and firm up. Then, divide the dough into three equally sized portions. Roll them into a ball. Next, on a baking sheet lined with parchment paper, press each of the dough balls into a round cookie, with a thickness of about 5 mm (about ¼ of an inch). They will each have a diameter of about 15-16 cm (6 inches.)

6. Brush the surface of the three cookies with the beaten egg. Then, sprinkle them evenly with some pearl sugar.

7. Bake for about 12-15 minutes until their surface becomes a light golden brown. Take them out of the oven and let them cool on the baking sheet for about 10 minutes. Next, transfer them carefully to a wire rack to cool completely. Store in an airtight container or wrapped in tinfoil.

A BIG, CRUMBLY COOKIE-LIKE PASTRY FROM GLARUS

Glarus is the Swiss canton with the smallest capital city, which carries the same name. On a day trip to the city of Glarus one year, I visited a number of bakeries in search of the *zeltes*–Drusenzelte and Ankenzelte. From my experience, you cannot find them anywhere else in the country, so I was on a mission to track them down.

These two round pastries both contain raisins, but have very different textures. The Ankenzelte is soft, while the Drusenzelte resembles a large crumbly cookie. The *zelte* in their name refers to flat pastries in the local dialect.

Butter is also something that they both have in common, but in distinctly different forms. For the Ankenzelte, the *anken* part of the name means 'butter.' In comparison, Drusenzelte contains the term *drusen*, a by-product from making butter. To preserve butter over the long term, people would boil it down. As they did this, and the water evaporated, milk proteins started collecting in the form of foam on the surface. To make clarified butter, these parts are skimmed off and separated from the mixture. If you continue to boil the butter, however, the milk proteins will sink to the bottom and start to brown—the method used to make ghee. When the milk proteins start to brown, they further develop their flavor. Patrimoine Culinaire Suisse describes them as "schwarze Krümel und schmecken caramelähnlich" ('black crumbs with a caramel-like taste'). It's these *drusen* that bakers once used to make the Drusenzelte in Glarus.

Today, bakeries in Glarus generally use butter or clarified butter, instead of *drusen*, to make these pastries. Although I tried making it several times with clarified butter, I now prefer using 100 percent regular, unsalted butter. If you would like to try adding in some clarified butter to this cookie dough, you can purchase it already made, or you can make it yourself.

This recipe works especially well for a quick afternoon snack. You can throw them together quickly with ingredients you likely have on hand. They taste best while still a bit warm and with a glass of milk. I also like replacing the raisins in this recipe with chocolate chips.

31 GRASSINS

Preparation Time
approx. 45 minutes
bake for 10-12 minutes

Quantity
Makes about 3-4 dozen cookies.

INGREDIENTS

- 170 g (3⁄4 cup) unsalted butter, softened
- 150 g (3⁄4 cup) sugar
- 1 tablespoon iva* or milk
- 250 g (2 cups) all-purpose flour
- ½ to 1 teaspoon salt

*Iva is a traditional liqueur made from alpine flowers in the Swiss canton of Graubünden. You can substitute this ingredient with another type of fruit or herbal schnapps or milk.

INSTRUCTIONS

1. Mix the butter and sugar together just until creamy and well blended. Then stir in the iva until it becomes completely incorporated into the mixture.

2. Separately, whisk together the flour and salt. Then, add it to the butter and sugar mixture, stirring it together just until a dough forms. Take the dough out of the bowl and form it into a flattened disk. Wrap the dough in parchment paper and refrigerate it for about 30 minutes.

3. On a floured surface and with a rolling pin dusted in flour, roll out the dough to about 5 mm thick (about ¼ of an inch). Using a small cookie cutter (diameter: about 3 cm / 1 ¼ inches), cut out circles or other shapes in the dough. Gently place them on a baking sheet lined with parchment paper.

4. Bake for about 10-12 minutes at 180°C / 350°F. Place on a wire rack to cool.

A SIMPLE BUTTER COOKIE THAT MELTS IN YOUR MOUTH

A traditional biscuit from the canton of Graubünden, Grassins are popular during the holiday season. You'll find them mainly in the Engadin region of this Swiss canton, where they have existed since at least the 19th century. While these biscuits may seem quite simple today, they were originally made during a time when white flour was considered a luxury item in this valley, reserved for special occasions. Grassins are typically round, but you may also find them in other shapes, such as hearts or stars.

Made with a short crust pastry, Grassins contain a lot of butter! The other main ingredients in these cookies include flour, sugar and salt. Some bakers will also add eggs—either a whole egg or just the yolk. I prefer them without egg, otherwise I find they too closely resemble another Swiss cookie for Christmas—the Mailänderli (recipe online via my blog), which always contains some egg in the dough, as well as a bright-yellow egg yolk wash on its surface.

The Grassins have endless variations—there are many ways you can add different ingredients to these cookies. For example, you could press a walnut into its surface before baking or you could add chopped dried cranberries to the dough. Via my blog, you'll also find a recipe for Grassins with a chocolate coin pressed into its surface immediately after it comes out of the oven.

For the recipe in this book, I have added iva, an alpine floral liqueur from the same canton. To make iva, you macerate flowers from the musk yarrow plant in alcohol, typically a brandy distilled from wine. The color of the drink ranges from clear to green to a light brown. Producers will add sugar to balance the bitter flavor of the iva blossoms. Its alcohol content generally ranges between 25-40 percent. I find that this lightly sweetened liqueur adds a delicate herbal flavor to the biscuits. If you don't have access to this uniquely Swiss spirit, I recommend another fruit or herbal brandy, or you can also use a tablespoon of milk instead.

When you need a basic cut-out cookie fast, with ingredients you already have in your kitchen, this is a great go-to recipe.

32 SEISLER BRÄTZELE

Preparation Time
at least 2 hours 30 minutes
cook for approx. 3-5 minutes

Quantity
Makes about 15-20 cookies.

Tools
Electric Bretzel / Bricelet iron

INGREDIENTS

- 250 ml (1 cup) double cream (45% milk fat)
- 1 tablespoon sugar
- ½ teaspoon salt
- 225 g (1 ¾ cups) all-purpose flour

INSTRUCTIONS

1. In a large bowl, whisk together the double cream, sugar and salt until well combined. Stir in the flour and when a dough starts to form, knead it together with your hands, or with a dough hook and an electric mixer. Continue kneading just until all the flour has been incorporated and it has become a smooth dough. Form the dough into a disk. Wrap it in parchment paper or place it in an airtight container. Refrigerate for at least two hours or overnight.

2. When the dough is ready, roll it out on a floured surface with a rolling pin lightly dusted with flour. Make a rectangle that measures about 23 x 33 cm (9 x 13 inches) lengthwise—the dough should be about 4-5 mm thick (about ¼ of an inch).

3. Using a pastry wheel or a knife, cut two long, thin strips in the dough, less than 1 cm wide (less than ½ inch). Bring the ends of the dough together to one of the strips, creating a long loop. Repeat this process with the rest of the dough, creating a series of long dough loops.

4. Prepare the electric Bretzel / Bricelet iron. When the iron is hot, lay one dough loop on the iron at an angle, and then quickly add a second loop, creating an X-shape. Close the iron over the dough and follow the directions for the machine in order to determine when it is done. It should take approximately 3 minutes to cook in the machine. When it has finished, remove it from the machine and place it on a wire rack to cool. Repeat this process with the remaining dough loops.

A SWEET & SALTY BISCUIT WITH A SPECIAL SHAPE

In the Sense district of Fribourg, an *apéro* (aperitif) with white wine might include a local specialty known as the Seisler Brätzele or Sensler Bretzel. This German-speaking district of the canton has historically enjoyed these biscuits during *chilbi* harvest celebrations in the fall. Cooked between a hinged baking iron, their shape does not seem to resemble any other Bretzel (Bricelet) found in Switzerland.

In the French-speaking parts of Fribourg, Bricelets for the *bénichon* celebrations (the French equivalent of *chilbi*) are rolled into cylinders and have a sweeter taste. You can find these thin biscuits in the canton of Bern as well—pressed into flat biscuits or rolled into cylinders. I have also had savory Bricelets in the canton of Neuchâtel, made with salt and caraway seeds, in addition to the classic sweet version. Sometimes the dough for Bricelets is thick and rolled into a ball before being placed on a baking iron. Other times, people use a batter that is poured onto the baking iron with a ladle.

The dough for these biscuits in Fribourg contains few ingredients. For my recipe, you simply knead together the following just until a dough forms: flour, double cream, sugar and salt. Some variations of this recipe can include other ingredients, and some Bricelets are sweeter than others. Generally, the ones from the Sense district are more salty than sweet.

The Seisler Brätzele has an X-shaped pattern with five holes. You bake it on a hinged baking iron, which presses the dough flat as it bakes. Using the traditional hinged irons, you can bake the biscuits in the embers of a fire or over the flames of a gas cooker. People have been making these biscuits since the 18th century, and the baking irons, recipes and know-how have been passed down through the generations.

When I make Seisler Brätzele at home, I use an electric Bretzel iron. Their unique shape makes them unlike any other biscuit or cracker that I have ever seen. Plus, with the double cream, they have a crisp, but tender texture. Crack open a bottle of white wine, break out these special biscuits and you've got a reason to celebrate.

33 SPITZBUBEN

Preparation Time

approx. 1 hour 15 minutes

bake for about 10 minutes

Quantity

Makes approx. 15 cookies.

INGREDIENTS

Dough

- 180 g (¾ cup + 2 teaspoons) unsalted butter
- 60 g (½ cup) powdered sugar
- 1 teaspoon vanilla extract or paste
- 145 g (1 cup + 2 ½ tablespoons) all-purpose flour
- 155 g (1 ⅓ cups) whole wheat flour
- ¼ teaspoon salt
- 1-2 tablespoons milk

Filling:

- Use your favorite jam or make your own strawberry jam (p. 46).

INSTRUCTIONS

1. In a large bowl, cream together the butter, powdered sugar and vanilla until the mixture is smooth and well combined. Set aside.

2. In another bowl, whisk together the all-purpose flour, whole wheat flour and salt.

3. Add the flour mixture to the ingredients in the large bowl and add 1-2 tablespoons of milk. Stir together just until a dough forms. Form the dough into a disk, wrap it in parchment paper and refrigerate for approximately 30-60 minutes.

4. On a lightly floured surface and with a lightly floured rolling pin (if the dough sticks to it), roll out the dough to a thickness of 3 mm (about 1/10 inch).

5. Place the cookies on a baking sheet lined with parchment paper. Use a smaller cookie cutter (or the opposite side of a piping tip, etc.) to make a window for the jam in half of the cookies. Half of your cookies should be 'base' cookies, and the other half should be 'window' cookies.

6. Bake for about 10 minutes at 180˚C / 350°F until the cookies have become firm and only lightly browned around the edges, if at all.

7. Let them cool for a few minutes on the baking sheet, and then place them on a wire rack to cool.

8. Once the cookies have completely cooled, prepare the 'window' cookies. My preference is to leave the surface of the 'window' cookies as is. Otherwise, you can either: (1) sprinkle them with some powdered sugar or (2) brush them with an icing made by whisking together 50 grams (about ½ cup) powdered sugar and 2 teaspoons of water or lemon juice.

9. On the 'base' cookies, spread about 1 teaspoon of jam on the cookie. Place the 'window' cookie on top. To store, layer these cookies with parchment paper in an airtight container.

SWITZERLAND'S VERSION OF THE LINZER COOKIE

You can find jammy, short-crust sandwich cookies in many countries around the world. In the United States, I would refer to these as 'Linzer' cookies, as they call them in Austria. Switzerland has its own version, of course, with different names in different linguistic regions.

I know them in Suisse Romande as Miroirs (mirrors) or Coquins—the French version of their Swiss German name, Spitzbuben. These names translate to something like 'rascal' or 'cheeky boy.' Although many theories exist, I have not yet run across a clear origin story for this name. At this time, the oldest documented recipe for these cookies comes from a 1929 cookbook entitled *Das Meisterwerk der Küche* (The Masterpiece of the Kitchen), as reported by Patrimoine Culinaire Suisse.

The top layer of the biscuit will often have three equidistant holes that would form a triangle if you drew a line between them. This design is especially popular at Christmastime. Sometimes the edges of the biscuits will be fluted, sometimes not. Throughout the year, you can still find Spitzbuben at bakeries and supermarkets. These will often have a smiling face cut into the top biscuit layer, which also has thin icing. The face looks a bit like the name of the biscuit personified on its surface. You will also find examples of these biscuits with just one cut-out in its center, such as a heart, star or just a round circle.

Frequently, Spitzbuben are filled with red jam, perhaps raspberry or red currant. You can make them with whatever jam you have on hand though. I have added whole wheat to my recipe, which is not traditional, but I think it adds more texture and flavor to the biscuit.

For Switzerland's National Day, I make these with a cut-out like the cross on the Swiss flag for a patriotic version of these 'rascal' cookies. Bottom line—these cookies are good any time of year, not just for Christmas, and are very satisfying to make for yourself.

34 TOTENBEINLI

Preparation Time
approx. 3 hours
bake for 15-20 minutes

Quantity
Makes approx. 40 cookies.

INGREDIENTS

Dough

- 200 g (1 ⅓ cups) whole hazelnuts
- 100 g (7 tablespoons) unsalted butter, softened
- 125 g (scant ⅔ cup) sugar
- 2 eggs
- 125 g (1 cup) all-purpose flour
- 125 g (1 cup + 1 tablespoon) whole wheat flour
- ½ teaspoon salt
- ½ teaspoon cinnamon
- ¼ teaspoon nutmeg
- ¼ teaspoon white pepper

Brush on top:

- 1 egg, beaten

INSTRUCTIONS

1. Toast the hazelnuts*. Preheat the oven to 180°C / 350°F. On a baking sheet lined with parchment paper, spread out the whole hazelnuts. When the oven is ready, place them in the oven for about 10-15 minutes. Bake just until the skins begin to break open. Remove the pan from the oven and wrap the hot hazelnuts in a kitchen towel (use an old towel, as it might become a bit stained). Let them sit for about 5-10 minutes and then rub the nuts together in your hands to loosen the skins. Peel them off as best as you can, but don't stress. They won't all completely come off. Remove the ones you can. Place the hazelnuts in a bowl and set them aside to cool.

   *I like toasting the hazelnuts to bring out their flavor and to remove their skins, which can have a slightly bitter taste. However, you can skip this step altogether and add the un-toasted hazelnuts with their skins to the cookie dough.

2. Make the dough. In a large bowl, cream together the butter and sugar. Add the two eggs and stir until well blended. Set aside.

3. In a separate bowl, whisk together the dry ingredients: the white and whole flours, salt, cinnamon, nutmeg and white pepper.

4. Add the dry ingredients to the large bowl with butter, sugar and eggs. Stir together just until the dry ingredients have been fully incorporated.

5. Mix the hazelnuts into the dough until they are well distributed. Place the dough on a piece of parchment paper dusted with flour. Using a rolling pin dusted with flour, roll out the dough into a rectangle that's about 1 cm thick (about ½ inch). Wrap the dough in parchment paper and place it in the refrigerator for about 1-2 hours or overnight.

6. When the dough has become firm, brush the top of the dough with the beaten egg. Then, with a very sharp knife, cut the chilled dough into strips about 1 cm by 10 cm (½ inch by 4 inches). Place them on a baking sheet lined with parchment paper and bake for approximately 15-20 minutes at 180°C / 350°F until their surface becomes golden brown. After letting them rest on the baking sheet for about 10 minutes, place them on a wire rack to fully cool. Store in an airtight container for about 2-3 weeks.

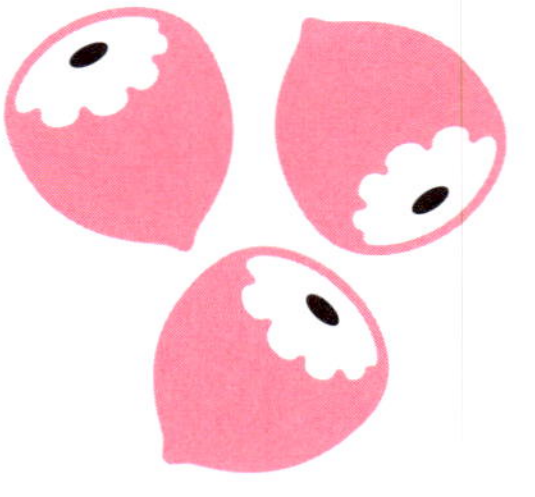

EATING 'LITTLE DEAD LEGS' WITH HAZELNUTS

Switzerland has a number of sweet treats named after legs. There are thick, elongated beignets known as Schenkeli (German) or Cuisse dames (French), which literally translated means 'women's thighs.' A U-shaped yeasted dough with a hazelnut filling, known as a Meitschibei, means 'girl's legs.' So, it should come to no surprise that a hazelnut cookie from Graubünden carries a name like Totenbeinli ('little dead legs').

A more benign way to refer to these cookies is simply as 'hazelnut sticks'—Nuss-Stängeli (Swiss German), Nuss-Stengel (in German), Bâtons aux noisettes (French) and Bastoncini (Italian).

The main ingredients for these biscuits are flour, sugar, hazelnuts, eggs and milk. They have a very hard consistency, almost like an Italian biscotti, except you only bake them once (although some bakers may bake them twice). With such a firm texture, they have a long shelf life. Their name comes from a tradition of them being served with coffee at funerals. No longer a cookie just for people in mourning, you can find Totenbeinli throughout the year, and especially during Christmastime.

You'll find lots of different recipes for these cookies. Mine calls for whole roasted hazelnuts. When you slice these hazelnut sticks, the halved hazelnuts appear along their sides. Perhaps it will remind you of a famous Swiss chocolate bar from the Jura?

Switzerland

35 ZIMTSTÄNGEL

Preparation Time

approx. 1 hour 30 minutes

bake for 8-10 minutes

Quantity

Makes approx. 60-70 biscuits.

INGREDIENTS

Dry ingredients:

- 200 g (2 ½ cups) ground almonds or hazelnuts
- 200 g (1 ½ cups + 1 tablespoon) all-purpose flour
- 2 tablespoons cocoa powder
- 2 teaspoons ground cinnamon
- 1 teaspoon baking powder
- ½ teaspoon salt
- ¼ teaspoon ground cloves

Wet ingredients:

- 250 g (1 ¼ cups) sugar
- 2 eggs
- 2 tablespoons kirsch (or milk)
- zest of one organic lemon

INSTRUCTIONS

1. In a large bowl, whisk together the dry ingredients: ground almonds, all-purpose flour, cocoa powder, cinnamon, baking powder, salt and cloves. Set aside.

2. Separately, in another large bowl, beat the sugar and eggs together until the mixture becomes a bit frothy and takes on a light-yellow color. Stir in the kirsch and lemon zest.

3. Add dry ingredients to the bowl with the wet ingredients and stir together until a dough forms. Cover the bowl and chill the dough in the refrigerator for about 1-2 hours.

4. When the dough is ready, on a surface lightly dusted with flour, roll it out into thin cylinders similar to the width of about 2 cm (¾ of an inch). Cut the cylinders into pieces about 5 cm (2 inches) long. Place them on a baking sheet lined with parchment paper. Gently press the cylinders down with your fingers to flatten them slightly. Then, take a sharp knife and make two diagonal slash marks across the width of the cookies. Sprinkle the cookies with a dusting of sugar.

5. Bake the cookies for about 8-10 minutes at 200˚C / 400˚F. When you take them out of the oven, they should be firm, but still a little soft when you touch them. Cool on a wire rack and store in an airtight container.

BASEL'S OTHER BROWN COOKIE

In northeast Switzerland, there are two Basel half-cantons: Basel-Stadt and Basel-Landschaft. A famous spiced chocolate cookie, popular during the Christmas season throughout the country, has a strong association with Basel-Stadt. This half-canton is where the city of Basel is located, and the little cut-out cookies are known as Basler Brunsli ('Basel's little browns').

The half-canton of Basel-Landschaft, a more rural area in comparison to the more urban Basel-Stadt, has another little brown biscuit. Literally translated, Zimtstängel means 'cinnamon stick.' While I don't have empirical evidence to support this, anecdotally I find that this biscuit has less recognition nationally than the Basler Brunsli.

Perhaps you could consider the Zimtstängel a bit of a combination between the Basler Brunsli and another popular Swiss Christmas cookie, the Zimtsterne (cinnamon star). Unlike these Christmas cookies however, the Zimtstängel is more of a year-round cookie. These cinnamon sticks contain cocoa or chocolate powder and can be made with almonds, hazelnuts or a combination of both. Their history reaches back to at least the first part of the 20th century in Basel-Landschaft.

Within the farming communities of this half-canton, when people would eat in the fields during the workday, Zimtstängel would be a portable and hearty snack. It reminds me of the stories my mother tells me about my grandmother's fortifying oatmeal cookies on the farm in Minnesota. When she was a child, she would bring these out to her father (my grandfather) when he was working in the fields. These kinds of cookies are everyday cookies, made for the people you love—to fill them up and keep them moving.

VI

CREAMY DESSERTS & OTHER SWEET TREATS

CRÈMES UND ANDERE LECKEREIEN

DESSERTS CRÉMEUX ET AUTRES GOURMANDISES

VI. CREAMY DESSERTS & OTHER SWEET TREATS

You will notice that this chapter has the fewest baked recipes in this book. The majority are actually stove-top recipes. These include a few of my favorite creamy puddings and frozen desserts. In addition, I share some snacks with texture, like meringues, candied walnuts and somewhat sandy caramels. These sweet little treats work well as homemade gifts, or perhaps crushed and sprinkled on the creamier desserts found in the following pages.

For some of the recipes, such as the Brönnti Crème with a butterscotch twist, I have made small adjustments to classic Swiss dishes. A few more rustic recipes also appear in this chapter, such as Cholermüs from Obwalden (p. 205) or Heiperchochchüechu from Valais (p. 209). A number of these dishes contain fresh (or frozen) fruit, such as cherries, plums and blueberries.

A major highlight for me in this chapter is most definitely the 5-part recipes from the Michelin-starred chef Bernadette Lisibach (p. 199). I am thrilled that she trusted me with her recipes, which feature some traditional sweet dishes from the cantons of St. Gallen and Thurgau. With apples in three different forms, this dessert is a showstopper!

36 BRÖNNTI CRÈME

Preparation Time
approx. 2 hours 30 minutes
chill for 2 hours

Quantity
Makes approx. 4-5 servings.

INGREDIENTS

- 500 ml (2 cups + 1 tablespoon) whole milk (3.5% milk fat)
- 15 g (about 2 tablespoons) cornstarch
- 1 tablespoon molasses
- 1 egg
- 1 egg yolk
- ½ teaspoon salt
- 100 g (½ cup) sugar
- 2 tablespoons water
- 1 lemon wedge
- 24 g (about 2 tablespoons) unsalted butter
- 150 ml (⅔ cup) heavy cream (35% milk fat)

INSTRUCTIONS

1. In a large bowl, whisk together the milk, cornstarch, molasses, egg, egg yolk and salt. Set aside.

2. Separately, add the sugar and water to a medium saucepan. Then, squeeze the lemon wedge, adding a splash of its juice to the saucepan. Over low to medium heat, let the sugar begin to caramelize and turn golden brown. Do not stir the mixture, but rather tilt the pan gently from time to time to swirl the mixture around in the pan, until the caramel color is evenly distributed. Watch the pan closely to make sure the sugar doesn't burn. Be patient – this can take about 30 minutes.

3. Take the pan off the heat when the mixture has a smooth consistency and a deep caramel color. Next, gently whisk in the butter. Then, whisk in the milk and egg contents of the large bowl, working quickly so the eggs don't start to cook into clumps. Once all the ingredients are well incorporated, return the saucepan to the burner, and let it simmer over low to medium heat, stirring frequently.

4. When the mixture has thickened and turned a light golden-brown color, remove it from the heat and continue stirring a bit more until it has a smooth texture. Pour the mixture into a heat-safe bowl, passing it through a sieve to remove any lumps from the mixture, and let it cool to room temperature. Cover the bowl and place it in the refrigerator to cool for at least two hours.

5. After the caramel cream has chilled, whip the heavy cream with an electric mixer until fluffy. Then, take the caramel cream out of the refrigerator and mix in about two-thirds of the whipped cream until it is evenly distributed.

6. To serve, use one large bowl or several small bowls for individual portions. Add the Brön-nti Crème, and then top with the remaining whipped cream.

   Optional garnish to sprinkle on top: toasted flaked almonds, crumbled Caramels à la crème (p. 217) or finely chopped Candied Walnuts (p. 221).

BURNT CREAM WITH A BUTTERSCOTCH TWIST

Brönnti Crème (Swiss German) or Gebrannte Crème (German) literally translated means 'burnt cream.' You may also see it called Karamelcrème. To be honest, I am not the kind of person that usually seeks out creamy desserts like this one. I generally avoid puddings, custards or even Cremeschnitten (a Swiss version of the Mille-feuille). After trying this recipe at home, however, and making a few adjustments, this has become one of my new favorite desserts.

Growing up in the United States, my only experience with creamy pudding came from a box. You would mix the powdered contents with milk for an instant dessert. Pudding always seemed to me like the kind of dessert you would get in a school or hospital cafeteria—an industrial, premade sweet treat.

The Swiss Brönnti Crème, by contrast, is made with fresh ingredients. This classic dessert is a caramelized sugar pudding, topped with a dollop of whipped cream. For my recipe, I have made a few adjustments so that it reminds me of American butterscotch pudding. Except this time it's 100 percent homemade.

I had not realized the 'Americanness' of butterscotch until my first visit to the St. Moritz Gourmet Festival in 2017. Chef Melissa Kelly, visiting from the US, prepared a Butterscotch Budino. Before, I had often avoided butterscotch because I felt it had a somewhat artificial taste. Chef Kelly's dessert, on the other hand, had an incredible and very real butterscotch flavor—salty and sweet in the best kind of way. Normally made with butter, brown sugar and some salt, butterscotch is a typically American flavor for candies, pudding, sauce and more. Chef Kelly told me she had to make her own version of a soft American brown sugar in Switzerland using molasses and white sugar. After that dinner, I gained a new appreciation for butterscotch!

When I started making Brönnti Crème at home, I remembered that meal in St. Moritz with Chef Kelly and added a butterscotch twist to this classic Swiss dessert. With the addition of butter, molasses and salt, it reminds me of the butterscotch flavor I had growing up, but without any artificial flavors. I have to say, it took a move to Switzerland for me to discover a truly American flavor, paired with the cooking techniques of a traditional Brönnti Crème.

37 CHOCOLATE PARFAIT GLACÉ À L'ABSINTHE

Preparation Time
approx. 1 hour
chill for at least 2 hours

Quantity
Makes about 5 servings.

INGREDIENTS

- 150 ml (⅔ cup) heavy cream (35% milk fat)
- 2 eggs
- 1 egg yolk
- 50 g (¼ cup) sugar
- 100 ml (scant ½ cup) light cream (25% milk fat)
- 75 g (2.6 ounces) dark chocolate, finely chopped
- 50-60 ml (3-4 tablespoons) absinthe

INSTRUCTIONS

1. In a large metal bowl, whip the heavy cream until it becomes fluffy and just until it creates stiff peaks. Put the whipped cream in the fridge to chill.

2. Separately, with an electric mixer, beat together the eggs, egg yolk and sugar for several minutes until the mixture becomes frothy and turns a pale-yellow color. Set aside. Bring the light cream to a rolling boil in a medium-sized saucepan and take it off the stove. Whisk in some of the boiling cream to the egg and sugar mixture vigorously, making sure that the egg does not start to curdle. Continue until all the light cream has been fully incorporated into the egg mixture. Return the mixture to the saucepan over low heat and gently simmer the mixture, while whisking it constantly for a few minutes until it starts to thicken and making sure the eggs don't start to curdle.

3. Once the mixture has thickened, take it off the stove and whisk the finely chopped chocolate into the mixture until it's fully melted and evenly distributed. Next, stir in the absinthe. Let the pan sit in ice water to cool the mixture to room temperature.

4. When the chocolate mixture has cooled, take the whipped cream out of the refrigerator and gently fold it into the mixture.

5. Carefully spoon the chocolate into 4-5 small jars, ramekins or glasses and place in the freezer for about 2-4 hours. The longer they stay in the freezer, the more time they may need at room temperature for the mixture to soften before serving. Garnish with fresh berries, chocolate, mint leaves and / or a dusting of cocoa powder.

A FROZEN CHOCOLATE-ABSINTHE MOUSSE

Before I moved to Switzerland, I had no idea of its connection to absinthe. Nor did I realize that the canton of Neuchâtel, where we were moving to, is considered the birthplace of this potent alcoholic beverage. One of the first desserts I tried with absinthe was the Parfait glacé à l'absinthe at Festin Neuchâtelois in 2013, a local feast that highlights culinary specialties from the canton. A traditional dish for this event's special menu, participating restaurants add their own special touches to this local dessert.

Also known as the Green Fairy and other various nicknames, like the Milk of Val-de-Travers, absinthe turns cloudy when you add water. It may have had a reputation as a toxic alcoholic beverage that makes you hallucinate, but residents of the Val-de-Travers have been drinking and cooking with it for centuries, and in some cases, with recipes that have been passed down for generations.

To be considered a true absinthe, it must have four key ingredients: small or Roman wormwood (Artemisia pontica), large wormwood (Artemisia absinthium), fennel and green anise. Thujone, a toxic component found in wormwood, supposedly induced hallucinogenic symptoms. In large quantities, thujone can indeed be detrimental to your health. However, the amount of today's absinthe you would have to drink to reach these toxic levels would likely kill you first from alcohol poisoning. Nevertheless, following a tragic incident in which a severely inebriated man, drunk on wine and absinthe, murdered his pregnant wife and two children, Swiss citizens voted in favor of an absinthe ban in 1908.

The former courthouse where Swiss absinthe distillers used to be prosecuted during the ban on this notorious alcoholic beverage now houses a museum devoted to the Green Fairy: the Maison de l'Absinthe in the charming village of Môtiers. During the ban from 1910 until 2005, absinthe production continued in secret, despite the potential consequences facing distillers if they were caught.

Philippe Martin, an award-winning absinthe distiller, has some fascinating anecdotes about growing up in the Val-de-Travers with a father who was a bootlegger. For example, as a child he would not usually be allowed to take a bath on rainy days because those were the best days for distilling. His father would place the copper stills in the bathtub, and the rain would help to dilute the smoke and smell of the distilling process, keeping it hidden from nosy neighbors and the local authorities.

One incident in particular has been credited with helping to soften hardline positions on the ban. It occurred when French President François Mitterrand visited the restaurant at the Hôtel du Peyrou in the city of Neuchâtel in 1983. The chef, Daniel Aimone, served him a Soufflé glacé à la fée made with absinthe. It caused a major political scandal, which led to a trial that lasted about two years. Although, at the trial the chef changed his story and said he used pastis, an anise-flavored liqueur traditionally from France, rather than absinthe, in his dessert. This event arguably contributed to a change in perspectives that ultimately led to the legalization of absinthe in Switzerland in 2005.

Today, no longer confined to the shadows, absinthe appears throughout the canton of Neuchâtel at culinary events, restaurants and of course, in private homes. In terms of cooking, you can use it in both sweet and savory dishes, but I particularly enjoy it in desserts.

Closely related to the famous frozen soufflé for the French president, is the Parfait glacé à la fée verte. You can find many recipes and variations for this dessert throughout the canton, but not typically with chocolate, as my recipe calls for. Some will freeze the creamy mixture into a rectangular shape, which you slice to serve. Other recipes, like mine, put the mixture into individually sized containers (I use leftover glass yogurt jars).

If you like the flavor of absinthe, you will certainly enjoy this light, cool and refreshing dessert made with a uniquely Swiss ingredient.

38 GRIESSAUFLAUF WITH CHERRIES

Preparation Time
approx. 30 minutes
bake for 35-40 minutes

Quantity
Makes 6-8 servings.

INGREDIENTS

- 750 ml (3 cups + 3 tablespoons) milk
- 125 g (¾ cup) semolina
- 25 g unsalted butter, softened
- 50 g (¼ cup) sugar
- 4 egg yolks
- zest of one organic lemon
- 1 teaspoon cinnamon
- ¼ teaspoon cardamom
- ¼ teaspoon coriander
- ¼ teaspoon salt
- 4 egg whites (and a pinch of salt)
- 450-500 g (3 ¾ to 4 cups) whole pitted cherries, fresh or frozen

INSTRUCTIONS

1. Prepare a ceramic baking dish by greasing it generously with butter. Set aside.

   Note: I use a round ceramic dish with a diameter of about 28 cm (11 inches). You may need to adjust the baking time, depending on the size of dish you use to make this recipe.

2. Add the milk to a medium saucepan and bring to a boil. Gently pour in the semolina and stir until it becomes evenly incorporated into the milk. Let this mixture simmer over medium heat for several minutes until it thickens. Remove the pan from the heat and set it aside to cool.

3. Separately, cream together the butter and sugar. Add the egg yolks and lemon zest, beating the mixture together until it becomes light and creamy. Next, add the cooled semolina and the spices and salt to the bowl and stir until well combined.

4. In another bowl, whip the egg whites together with a pinch of salt until they are fluffy and form stiff peaks. Fold them into the large bowl with the other ingredients. Then, gently stir in the cherries until they are evenly distributed. Pour the mixture into the prepared ceramic baking dish.

5. Bake for about 35-40 minutes at 200°C / 400°F until the top becomes golden brown and the filling has set. Serve warm or cold with a dusting of powdered sugar.

A CHERRY CASSEROLE INSPIRED BY AN OLD ZUGER RECIPE

When you think of Zug and desserts, the Zuger Kirschtorte may immediately come to mind. Or, you may be familiar with the Räbentorte from Baar, a favorite of actress Sophia Loren. These two fantastic cakes have their roots in bakeries, so I wanted to introduce another recipe from the canton, more common with home bakers.

All over the German-speaking side of Switzerland, not just in Zug, there is a category of dishes with the suffix, *-auflauf.* When you see this ending, it means a baked dish, either sweet or savory. Loosely translated, it could be described as a casserole.

With regard to the sweet versions of Auflauf, they often contain fruit, and in particular stone fruit, such as plums, apricots and cherries. The canton of Nidwalden has an apple version, known as Apfelauflauf. You are more likely to see these dishes baked in a ceramic dish or perhaps even a cast iron pan. Eggs are also a key ingredient, but there are no set rules, so lots of different recipes exist under this category. Even though they contain fruit, these dishes can even masquerade as a main dish for a meal, especially if they contain little to no sugar.

After considering all the different types of Auflauf, I decided to focus on the versions of this Swiss casserole that contains *griess* (semolina)—the purified middlings of a hard wheat, such as durum. People use golden-hued semolina flour for making pasta. In addition to Auflauf, I have used semolina when making an Osterfladen, a classic Swiss Easter tart (you can find a recipe on my blog).

Once I had narrowed down semolina as a key ingredient for my Auflauf, I came across what is currently considered one of the oldest cherry recipes in Zug. Dating back to the late 18th century, researchers came across it in a collection of recipes currently held by the Bürgergemeinde Baar (Baar's municipal government). Named the Türkenbund (also Türggenbund), the *Schweizerisches Idiotikon* describes it as a "Hausmütze, wie sie Männer und Knaben ehedem zu tragen pflegten" (a type of house hat worn by boys and men). This term, meaning "Turkish hat," has also historically been used to describe a fluted cake with a hole in its center, the Hefegugelhopf. The name implies that the shape of the cake somehow resembles this type of hat, round and somewhat tall.

This historic Türkenbund recipe from Zug was adapted for today's kitchens and shared via the association, IG Zuger Chriesi. Started in 2008, the organization helps to preserve and promote the tradition of cherries in Zug. Over the years, it has planted a thousand cherry trees around the canton. In addition, it provides support to the *chriesimärt*, an annual cherry market that was first mentioned in 1627. This and other events, such as the *chriesisturm*, a race in which runners carry 8-meter-long cherry ladders through town, take place in June and July during peak cherry season.

My version of the Griessauflauf contains cherries—inspired by the reinvention of this historic recipe. It more closely resembles a cherry clafoutis and has a higher percentage of semolina than the original recipe. Instead of a tall round shape, I give this casserole a wider, more shallow form. I like it best served warm, but it also tastes good cold. You might want to sprinkle it with a dusting of powdered sugar and perhaps serve it with a glass of Zuger kirsch.

39 APPLE MERINGUE WITH SÜSSMOSTCREME, RUM RAISIN ICE CREAM AND HÜPPEN

From Bernadette Lisibach, Neue Blumenau in Lömmenschwil (St. Gallen)

APPLE MERINGUE

Preparation Time

approx. 4 hours 30 mins

bake for 4 hours

Quantity

Makes approx. 3 servings.

INGREDIENTS

- 15 g (1 tablespoon) unsalted butter
- 10 g (2-3 teaspoons) sugar
- 200 g Elstar apples (or another type of apple for baking)
- 75 g (about ½ quince) quince, poached
- 2 tablespoons quince or apple juice

Meringue topping

- 2 egg whites (80 g)
- a pinch of salt
- 160 g (¾ cup) sugar

INSTRUCTIONS

1. Line a small rectangular baking pan with parchment paper. Grease the parchment paper with the butter.

2. Peel and core the apples and cut into cubes. Peel the poached quince and cut into cubes. Gently toss the fruit with the sugar and quince (or apple) juice.

3. Add the fruit to the prepared pan, cover with aluminum foil and bake at 130°C / 250°F degrees for about 4 hours, or until the fruit becomes soft.

4. On the baking sheet, form the fruit into three round, flat bases for the meringue topping. If possible, use pastry rings for this purpose to hold the fruit together. Place the fruit back into the oven to keep it warm.

5. Prepare the meringue topping. Add the egg whites to a bowl with a pinch of salt and whip them with an electric mixer until frothy and they form stiff peaks. Then, continue to whip them while gradually adding in the sugar, about 1 tablespoon at a time, until the mixture becomes glossy.

6. Gently top the baked apple and quince bases with the meringue topping and broil in the oven until it browns a bit on top.

THURGAUER SÜSSMOSTCREME

Preparation Time

approx. 2 hours 30 minutes
refrigerate for 2 hours

Quantity

Makes approx. 2-4 servings.

INGREDIENTS

- 250 ml (1 cup) *süssmost* (apple cider)
- 2 teaspoons lemon juice
- 3 egg yolks (50 g)
- 50 g (¼ cup) sugar
- 1½ sheets gelatin
- 100 g (¼ cup + 3 tablespoons) heavy cream (35% milk fat)

INSTRUCTIONS

1. Add the *süssmost* and lemon juice to a medium-sized saucepan and bring to a boil.

2. Separately, whisk together the egg yolks and sugar. Take the saucepan off the heat and gradually add the egg yolk and sugar mixture to the pan, whisking constantly until well combined to avoid the egg from curdling.

3. Return the pan to the stove, and heat the mixture to 85˚C / 185˚F. While the mixture is heating up, soak the gelatin in cold water until it softens. Squeeze out the excess water. Add the gelatin to a small saucepan and gently heat until it melts. Whisk a small amount of the mixture in a small saucepan until well combined. Then, add the gelatin to the egg mixture in the medium-sized saucepan and whisk together until completely incorporated

4. Pour the mixture into a bowl and let it cool until it reaches room temperature. Then, refrigerate the mixture for at least 2 hours. Whip the heavy cream until it becomes light and fluffy, and then fold it into the apple cream.

RUM RAISIN ICE CREAM

Preparation time

at least 5 hours
refrigerate for 2 hours

Quantity

Makes approx. 2-4 servings.

INGREDIENTS

- 30 g (3 tablespoons) raisins
- 2 tablespoons rum
- 350 g (1 ½ cups) whole milk (3.5% milk fat)
- 1 vanilla bean
- 5-6 egg yolks (100 g)
- 50 g (¼ cup) sugar
- 150 g (⅔ cup) heavy cream (35% milk fat)

INSTRUCTIONS

1. Soak the raisins in rum for several hours or overnight.

2. Once the raisins have softened, start to make the ice cream. Add the whole milk and vanilla pod to a medium saucepan and bring to a boil. While this milk is heating up, beat together the egg yolks and the sugar until well-combined and the mixture becomes a pale-yellow color. When the milk has started to boil, take it off the heat and quickly whisk in a thin, slow stream of the egg-sugar mixture, taking care not to

allow the egg yolks to solidify. Return the saucepan to the stove and heat the mixture to 72°C / 160°F. Next, stir the heavy cream into the mixture.

3. Let the mixture cool to room temperature, and then refrigerate it for at least 2 hours or overnight.

4. Add the mixture to an ice cream machine and follow the machine's instructions. During the last few minutes in the machine, add the rum-soaked raisins to the mixture. Store ice cream in the freezer in an air-tight container.

HÜPPEN

Preparation time
approx. 30 minutes
bake for 5 minutes

Quantity
Makes approx. 20 cookies.

INGREDIENTS

- 1 egg white (30 g)
- 30 g (2 tablespoons) powdered sugar
- 30 g (¼ cup) all-purpose flour
- 30 g (2 tablespoons) unsalted butter, melted and cooled

INSTRUCTIONS

1. Whip the eggs white together with powdered sugar until the mixture becomes light and frothy. Sift the flour over the mixture and carefully fold it in. Next, gently add the liquid butter, mixing until well-combined.

2. Using a pencil, draw leaf-like shapes about 5 cm (2 inches) wide and 7-8 cm (3 inches long) onto the backside of a piece of parchment paper. Spread about 1 teaspoon of the mixture thinly within the forms you created.

3. Carefully place the parchment paper onto a baking sheet. Bake for 5 minutes at 170°C / 340°F.

4. Immediately after you take them out of the oven, wrap each individual cookie around a wooden dowel (like the handle of a wooden spoon). One at a time, press the cookie as you roll it around the dowel, so it sticks together. The cookies are hot so be careful not to burn yourself! You need to work quickly because once they start to cool, they begin to break more easily as you roll them. Gently remove the cylindrical-shaped biscuit from the dowel and let it cool on a wire rack. Store in an air-tight container.

CANDIED APPLE

Preparation Time
approx. 15 minutes

Quantity
Makes approx. 10-15 candied apple balls.

INGREDIENTS

- 1-2 Elstar apples (or another firm apple for cooking)
- 100 ml (¼ cup + 3 tablespoons) water
- 30 g (scant 2 ½ tablespoons) sugar
- 1 tablespoon grenadine syrup

INSTRUCTIONS

1. Cut the apple into spheres with a small melon baller tool. You should aim for at least 10-15 balls of apple.

2. Bring the water, sugar and grenadine syrup to a boil.

3. Simmer the apple in the mixture for about 10 minutes until the pieces soften and the flesh takes on a reddish color.

4. Remove the apple spheres from the liquid with a slotted spoon and drain them.

A SWISS APPLE DESSERT FIT FOR MICHELIN-STARRED DINING

I first met Chef Bernadette Lisibach in 2020 at one of the first culinary events I attended following the first lockdown during the Covid-19 pandemic. At the historic Bellevue Palace hotel in Bern, the winners were announced for the inaugural edition of the Mérite Culinaire Suisse. Organized by the Fondation pour la Promotion du Goût in Lausanne, this award honors chefs for their exceptional work and expertise, as well as their respect for local products that are part of Switzerland's culinary heritage. For its first year, the jury—composed of highly regarded chefs and journalists—selected a total of five winners, one of which was the talented chef working in the canton of St. Gallen, Chef Lisibach.

The second time I met Chef Lisibach, who is originally from the canton of Luzern, it was at a meeting of the Grandes Tables de Suisse at the Restaurant des Trois Tours in Bourguillon (Fribourg). As a member of the association, she was there to help recognize the outgoing president while welcoming the new one. She is one of the few female chefs working in Switzerland that belong to this association. In 2015, Gault Millau named her the country's Chef of the Year.

During the 10th anniversary of her restaurant, Neue Blumenau in Lömmenschwil, my boys and I had lunch out in the garden. Seated under a large arbor with a natural ceiling of green ivy and wisteria branches, it was their first meal at a Michelin-starred restaurant. Chef Lisibach visited all the tables to talk with the guests, many of whom seemed like regulars. I had a wonderful lunch together with my kids, and the dessert with local cherries, vanilla ice cream and a thin lattice of crisp biscuits balanced on top was particularly special.

When I asked Chef Lisibach about sharing a recipe for this book, she immediately mentioned that apples would likely be the central ingredient. The choice reflects an obvious nod to the region where she works. Her restaurant is located near the border with the canton of Thurgau, where they say one in every three Swiss apples is grown. I graciously thanked her for the wonderful meal and waited patiently to see what recipe I would ultimately receive.

Several weeks later, I got an email from her with a dessert recipe handwritten in German with five different components. To be honest, I wondered how I could pull this off. One by one, I translated the recipes and tested them in my home kitchen, adding additional instructions for home cooks where needed. Each worked perfectly the first time I made them!

It should also be mentioned that two of the five recipes stand out as being particularly Swiss: the *süssmostcreme*, an apple-cider pudding, and the *hüppen*, a cookie cylinder. Süssmostcreme has a strong link with home kitchens, and particularly the image of a grandmother making this dessert for her family. The *hüppen*, in comparison, exists almost exclusively in the professional sector. While Chef Lisibach's recipe does not call for any filling, these small, cylindrical biscuits are usually filled with chocolate. These dishes have strong regional identities, but you can find them in many parts of Switzerland. I loved the way she incorporated these traditional elements into one elegant dessert that remains accessible for amateur cooks.

What a pleasure I had plating this dessert with the five components all together. First, the roasted apple and quince cubes with a toasted meringue topping, resting in a shallow pool of *süssmostcreme* and surrounded by candied apple pieces tinted light red from the grenadine syrup. Finally, a crisp *hüppen* nestled next to a *quenelle* of homemade rum raisin ice cream (my mom's favorite). When you make this dish, you feel for one fleeting moment like a Michelin-star chef! Plus, the beauty of this recipe is that all the components can also work well on their own—if you don't want to tackle everything at once.

I was a fan of Chef Lisibach before, but my appreciation of her has grown exponentially with these great recipes and this fantastic multifaceted dessert.

NEUE BLUMENAU

Romanshornerstrasse 2
9308 Lömmenschwil
+41 (0)71 298 35 70
info@neueblumenau.ch
neueblumenau.ch

40 CHOLERMÜS

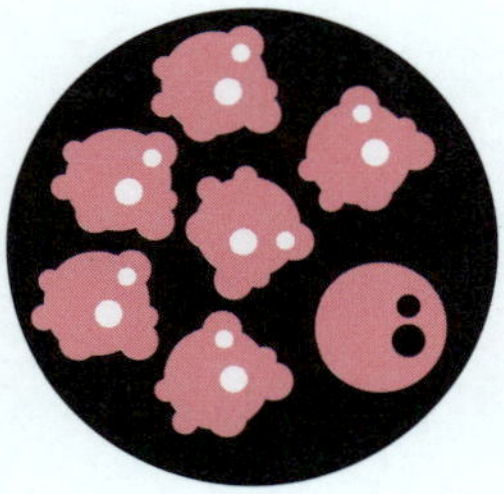

Preparation Time

approx. 45 minutes
cook for 15-20 minutes

Quantity

Makes 3-4 servings.

INGREDIENTS

- 3 eggs
- 250 ml (1 cup) light cream (25% milk fat)
- ½ teaspoon vanilla extract or paste
- 3 tablespoons sugar
- 175 g (1 ⅓ cup + 1 tablespoon) all-purpose flour
- ½ teaspoon cinnamon
- a pinch of nutmeg
- a pinch of salt
- 25-30 g (2 tablespoons) unsalted butter
- powdered sugar, to sprinkle on top

INSTRUCTIONS

1. Add the eggs to a large bowl and beat them together until frothy. Whisk in the light cream, sugar and vanilla until well combined. Set aside.

2. In a separate bowl, whisk together the dry ingredients: flour, cinnamon, nutmeg and salt. Then, add them to the bowl with the egg mixture and whisk everything together to create a smooth batter.

3. Let the batter rest for about 30-60 minutes at room temperature.

4. On the stove, melt 1 tablespoon of butter in a medium-sized frying pan. Swirl it around the bottom and the sides to help make sure the batter does not stick.

5. Pour the batter into the pan and let it cook over medium heat for about 10 minutes. When the bottom of the pancake has started to set, but the surface of the pancake is still a bit wet, roughly cut up the pancake into bite-size pieces with a spatula. Then, add the second tablespoon of butter to the pan. Fry the pancake pieces on all sides over medium-high heat until they turn golden brown.

6. Serve immediately, while still a little warm, with applesauce, stewed plums or jam. Optional: Dust the warm Cholermüs with powdered sugar.

OBWALDEN'S CHOPPED PANCAKE WITH APPLESAUCE

The Austrian Kaiserschmarrn may have better recognition in Switzerland than its cousin from Obwalden, Cholermüs. Some sources also connect it to Nidwalden, the other half-canton that previously made up the historic canton known as Unterwalden. These chopped stove-top pancakes work well almost any time of day. You can make one for breakfast, brunch or an afternoon snack.

Awareness of this relatively unknown chopped pancake grew, both inside and outside of Switzerland, after it was mentioned on the American television program, *The Big Bang Theory*, in 2010. In the episode, Sheldon mentions Cholermüs in preparation for an upcoming trip to Switzerland. Since it is a highly regional dish, it was a surprising choice for the program to mention it. They made one mistake, however, suggesting that it was traditionally a breakfast dish. In fact, people in Obwalden usually made this dish in the evening for dinner.

Unlike Kaiserschmarrn, you make Cholermüs primarily with cream instead of milk. Another Swiss chopped pancake from Graubünden, known as Tatsch, more closely resembles the Austrian version. I have tried both sweet and savory versions of Tatsch, another quick and versatile dish (you can find a sweet recipe on my blog).

Served with a dusting of powdered sugar and some applesauce or another fruit compote, Cholermüs is a satisfying rustic dish that fills you up. One of these days, I hope to solve the mystery and find out why the writers of *Big Bang Theory* selected it, out of all the Swiss dishes, to talk about on their show.

41 HEIPERCHOCHCHÜECHU

Preparation Time
approx. 30 minutes
cook for 20-30 minutes

Quantity
Makes one pancake.
2-3 servings

INGREDIENTS

- 20 g (1 ½ tablespoons) unsalted butter
- 6 tablespoons all-purpose flour (divided)
- 2 tablespoons light cream (25% milk fat)
- 2 tablespoons honey
- zest of one organic lime (or half a lemon)
- 150 g (1 cup) blueberries, fresh or frozen
- 1 tablespoon sugar
- 3 eggs
- 2 tablespoons milk

Sprinkle on top:

- 1 tablespoon sugar mixed with a generous pinch of cinnamon

INSTRUCTIONS

1. Melt the butter in a medium-sized frying pan over medium heat and then add 3 tablespoons of flour to the pan without stirring. Let the flour cook gently over the heat until it takes on a light golden-brown color.

2. Separately, whisk the light cream, honey and lime zest mixture together and add them to the fry pan with the blueberries once the flour has lightly browned. Bring the mixture to a boil and simmer for 1-2 minutes.

3. Next, whisk together the 3 tablespoons of flour and the sugar. Then, whisk in the 3 eggs and the milk. Make sure the blueberries are well-distributed in the frying pan, and then add the egg mixture to it. Cook over a low heat for about 15-20 minutes until the pancake becomes firm. Sprinkle it with cinnamon and sugar. Serve warm.

A BLUEBERRY SKILLET PANCAKE FROM VALAIS

German-speaking Valais has a rustic blueberry pancake with a long name. Known as Heiperchochchüechu, this pancake contains few ingredients and could almost be described as a sweet omelet. Its incredibly unpronounceable Swiss German name (at least for this American), can be broken into parts to determine its meaning. *Heipe* refers to the blueberries in this dish, *choch* means 'cook', and *chüechu* is a regional word for 'cake'.

With Swiss German largely a spoken and not written language, this also poses a particular challenge when attempting to spell the name of this dish phonetically. The first part sounds a bit like “hyper." After that, it gets more complicated! Following a phone call with someone who grew up in German-speaking Valais, I have given up on developing a pronunciation guide for this word. This person even told me that the way he pronounces this word differs from another area within this same region! Luckily, Heiperchochchüechu tastes just as good no matter how you say it.

42 MERINGUES

Preparation Time
approx. 15 minutes
bake for 2 hours

Quantity
Makes approx. 12 meringues.

INGREDIENTS

- 3 egg whites (about 120 g), room temperature
- a pinch of salt
- 170 g (¾ cup + 1 tablespoon) sugar

INSTRUCTIONS

1. In a large bowl, add the egg whites and a pinch of salt. Using an electric mixer with a whisk attachment, beat the egg whites until they become fluffy and form stiff peaks. Then, while the electric mixer is running, slowly add the sugar, about one tablespoon at a time, for about 4-5 minutes until it becomes well combined. The mixture should be thick and glossy.

2. Fold over the top half of the piping bag fitted with a piping tip.* Next, gently scoop the egg white mixture into the bag. Fold the top of the piping bag and twist it, so the mixture pushes down toward the tip. From the top of the bag, gently push the mixture through the piping tip onto a baking sheet with parchment paper to make approximately 12 meringues with a length about about 9 cm (3 ½ inches) and a width of no more than 5 cm (2 inches).

3. Put the meringues in an oven heated to 100°C / 200°F. Prop the oven door open with a wooden spoon to let the steam escape, which allows the meringues to fully dry out. Bake them for 2 hours, so that they have a firm texture.

*For this recipe, I use a 13 or 15 mm (almost ½ to ⅔ inch) open star tip. If you don't have or don't want to use a piping bag, just use two spoons to create 5-8 cm (2-3 inch) meringue dollops onto a baking sheet lined with parchment paper.

THE CLASSIC SIMPLICITY OF SWISS MERINGUES

Switzerland loves its version of meringues, with their rippled appearance and their dry, crisp and firm texture. I have had many people tell me that meringues are one of their favorite Swiss desserts. Swiss people generally serve their meringues with cream, but depending on where you are in the country, from my experience, the cream may take on a different form.

In French-speaking Switzerland, particularly in Fribourg, meringues come with a thick double cream, and in particular, *double crème de la Gruyère*. When you have meringues at someone's house or at a restaurant, you drizzle them with some double cream or perhaps dip them in the cream. This dessert may seem overly simplistic to some, but the sweet crisp meringues with the rich double cream make an ideal combination. When in season, fresh berries may also be served with this dish, or perhaps a scoop of ice cream. The main partner though, is the double cream. In Fribourg, and in my opinion, nearly all of French-speaking Switzerland, you really cannot have meringues without double cream. My friend from Gruyère always tells me that I am not taking enough, so I think of her whenever I have meringues and add more cream than I normally would!

Across the Röstigraben, in the canton of Bern, I find that the tradition of serving meringues with double cream is less pronounced. A more common pairing would be whipped cream or ice cream or both, which was my experience at Frutal's Tea Room in Meiringen. In fact, a popular legend claims the Bernese town of Meiringen as the birthplace of Swiss meringues. Centuries ago, an Italian chef named Gasparini, who worked in Meiringen, is said to have borrowed the name of the town for his new creation made of leftover egg whites and sugar. At the same time, meringue may have its origin in a country other than Switzerland, as multiple theories exist for how they started. Their invention by Gasparini appears to be one of the leading explanations for the name. However, the documented evidence for this link, once housed in a culinary museum in Frankfurt, Germany, was apparently destroyed in a fire during World War II.

Whether you serve your meringues with a bowl of thick double cream or a fluffy cloud of whipped cream, their crisp texture marries well with either form of this dairy product. I have fond memories of an Emmentaler restaurant where the dessert combined meringues with caramel-hued Brönnti Crème (recipe, p. 187) and vanilla ice cream. Another popular match for meringues and whipped cream are vermicelles, noodle-like strands of pureed chestnuts mixed with cream and sugar. One time, I had meringues with double cream after a cheese fondue lunch at an ephemeral outdoor table in the center of Lausanne. Meringues for dessert, and especially homemade ones, are a memorable occasion! I never thought I would ever attempt to make a Swiss-style meringue, but with a little practice, you can learn to make them yourself.

43 CARAMELS À LA CRÈME

Preparation Time
approx. 1 hour
cool for several hours

Quantity
Makes approx. 2-3 dozen caramels.

INGREDIENTS

- 200 g (1 cup) sugar
- 150 g (2/3 cup) double cream (45% milk fat)
- 100 g (1/4 cup + 3 tablespoons) heavy cream (35% milk fat)
- 1/2 teaspoon vanilla paste or extract
- 1/4 teaspoon salt

INSTRUCTIONS

1. Line a baking sheet with parchment paper. Set aside.

2. In a large saucepan, whisk together all the ingredients until well combined and bring them to a rolling boil, stirring frequently. When the volume of the mixture increases to about double its size, remove the pan from the heat.

3. Turn the temperature down to medium-low heat, return the pan to the stove and let the mixture simmer for about 30-45 minutes, stirring occasionally with a whisk. Watch the mixture closely so it does not start to burn. When the mixture thickens, becomes a bit foamy, turns a golden brown and starts to pull away from the sides of the pan, remove it from the heat and continue stirring for a few minutes more.

4. Pour the caramel onto the cookie sheet lined with parchment paper. Place another sheet of parchment paper on top, and then lay another baking sheet or pan on top of the parchment paper. Let the caramel cool like this for about 5-10 minutes.

5. With a sharp knife, slice the caramel into squares. Then, cover with a piece of parchment paper and allow them to cool completely for several hours. Separate the caramels and store them in a sealed container.

AN IRRESISTIBLE CARAMEL AND GLUTEN-FREE CANDY

The golden-brown caramel bubbled vigorously in the large copper pot. A whisk lay motionless in the pot, to be picked up from time to time and used to stir the sweet mass. Beside the pot were trays where the thickened caramel had been poured. It had been cut into rectangular pieces and left to cool. Visitors to the Salon Suisse des Goût & Terroirs in Bulle (Fribourg), a major culinary event held annually, could purchase bags of these irresistible Caramels à la crème to take home.

In the United States, the caramels that I was used to eating, both homemade and from commercial kitchens, needed to be individually wrapped because of their soft and sometimes sticky texture. In contrast, the caramels made in Fribourg, Vaud and other parts of Suisse Romande, can have a more granular texture. These types of caramels will not always include butter as an ingredient. The ones from Fribourg in particular can include double cream, and especially the *double crème* from Gruyère.

The recipes for these caramels, like all the others I consulted in Switzerland, do not contain any indication for using a candy thermometer. You have to just go by visual cues to determine when the caramel is 'done.' As such, I find that every time I make it always has some slight differences in color, texture and flavor.

For my recipe, I use a mixture of double cream and heavy cream. There are so many ways to change this recipe. You can add different spices or flavoring to the caramel mixture, such as cinnamon or splash of absinthe. Or, you could add chopped nuts to the caramel once it has thickened and right before you pour it out to cool. One of my favorite ways is to chop American candy canes during Christmas and sprinkle them on the surface of the caramels while they are still warm.

In German-speaking Switzerland, caramels carry names that range from Rahmtäfeli and Nidletäfeli to Nidlezeltli. They can vary in terms of their texture, color and ingredients. Some call for condensed milk or perhaps some cocoa powder. In Appenzell, the Nidlezeltli has a dark and very hard texture.

Homemade caramels make an excellent gift, particularly around the holidays, and also for family and friends who avoid gluten. Just make sure to save a few for yourself!

44 CANDIED WALNUTS WITH MAGENTRÄS

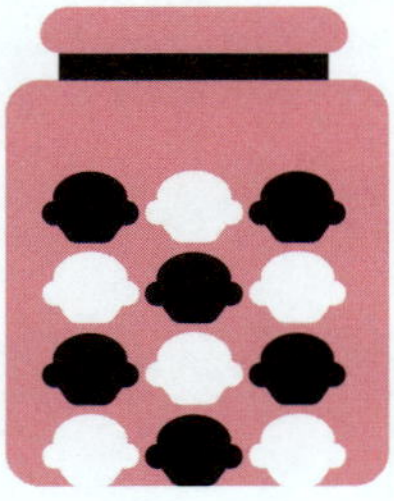

Preparation Time

approx. 30 minutes

Quantity

Makes about 250 grams (2 ½ cups).

INGREDIENTS

- 150 g (1 ½ cups) walnuts
- 130 g (⅔ cup) sugar
- 75 ml (⅓ cup) water
- 1 tablespoon rum
- 1 teaspoon *magenträs* (or ¼ teaspoon cinnamon)
- a pinch of salt

INSTRUCTIONS

1. First toast the walnuts in the oven. Place them on a cookie sheet lined with parchment paper and then in an oven preheated to 180˚C / 350˚F for about 5-10 minutes until they become fragrant. Take them out of the oven and let them cool.

2. When the toasted walnuts have cooled completely, add the other ingredients except the walnuts to a medium saucepan. Stir frequently and bring this mixture to a boil.

3. As soon as the mixture starts to boil, carefully add the walnuts. Reduce the temperature to medium heat.

4. Stir constantly with a large heat-safe spoon, until the liquid mixture begins to evaporate and crystallize.

5. Keep stirring, as the sugar will start to melt again. Once the walnuts have become lightly coated in the melted spiced sugar mixture, take them off the heat. Please note: It's very easy to overcook or even to burn the sugar mixture, so please be careful. If it overcooks, the coating on the walnuts will become too hard. Also, don't worry if some of the crystallized sugar gets caught in the crevices of the walnuts and does not melt. Just try and make sure all the smooth surfaces get lightly coated.

6. Pour the coated walnuts from the pot onto a baking sheet lined with parchment paper. The walnuts will be very hot. Be careful! Use the spoon to separate the walnuts that have stuck together.

7. Once the nuts have completely cooled, store them in a sealed container.

IRRESISTIBLE 'BURNT' WALNUTS WITH SPICED SANDALWOOD SUGAR

As the temperatures start to cool and fall festivals and eventually Christmas markets fill the streets, you will start seeing vendors selling bags of Gebrannte Mandeln (literally translated, 'burnt almonds'). These candied nuts have a sweet, crunchy texture, which goes well with a glass of *glühwein* (hot mulled wine).

Inspired to try making them at home, I came across a handful of recipes online that call for *sandelholzpulver* (sandalwood powder). Before moving to Switzerland, I had absolutely no experience using this as an ingredient in my cooking or baking. Since then, however, I have come to know sandalwood powder as a key component of one of my favorite Swiss food products, *magenträs*. So, I decided to come up with my own recipe for these candied nuts using this traditional Swiss ingredient.

Magenträs means 'stomach powder' in Swiss German dialect. Centuries ago, spiced sugars were used for medicinal purposes, and more specifically, to help with digestion. In addition to sugar and sandalwood powder, *magenträs* can also contain cinnamon, vanilla sugar, nutmeg, cloves and ginger. The sandalwood sugar has a unique flavor—slightly sweet with aromatic spices. The sandalwood powder helps give it a slightly reddish or coral color.

The largest producer of *magenträs* has its headquarters in Glarus, so it has a close connection to the culinary heritage of this canton. The peach-colored packet of this product, which features a boy holding a slice of bread—a popular vehicle for this product—has not changed in about 100 years.

For my candied nut recipe, I use walnuts instead of almonds, but you can certainly use whichever tree nut you prefer. Also, if you cannot find *magenträs* or even sandalwood powder very easily, you can add some cinnamon or your own personal blend of spices instead. Gebrannte Walnuts taste great on their own, as a homemade gift for family and friends. I especially like them chopped up and sprinkled on Zineb Hattab's frosted vegan carrot cake (p. 105).

45 PLUM SORBET WITH ROSEMARY AND DAMASSINE AOP

Preparation Time
approx. 3 hours
cool for 2+ hours

Quantity
Makes 6-8 servings.

INGREDIENTS

- 115 ml (½ cup) water
- 3 tablespoons honey
- About 550 g (1 ¼ lb) fresh or frozen Damasson rouge plums (or another variety), halved and pitted
- 1 sprig fresh rosemary
- 1 teaspoon lemon juice
- 1-2 tablespoons Damassine AOP (or another fruit-based schnapps / eau de vie)

INSTRUCTIONS

1. Add the water and honey to a medium-sized saucepan and stir until the honey dissolves in the liquid. Next, add the plums, rosemary and lemon juice. Bring the mixture to a boil and then simmer for about 15-30 minutes, until the plums have softened.

2. Take the pan off the heat. Remove the rosemary from the pan and let the mixture cool for a few minutes. Use an upright or immersion blender to puree the plum mixture until it becomes smooth. Whisk in the Damassine AOP. When the mixture has cooled to room temperature, cover it and place in the refrigerator to cool for at least two hours or preferably overnight.

3. Add the pureed plum mixture to an ice cream machine and follow the directions for the machine to make the sorbet. When it is ready, serve immediately, if desired, or store in an airtight container in the freezer.

A REFRESHING INTERLUDE DURING THE FEAST OF SAINT MARTIN

The Feast of Saint Martin, an event that centers around pork in many forms, takes place in the Jura canton. Born in Hungary, Saint Martin is known as the patron saint of France. The legend goes that while he was a soldier, upon meeting a beggar, he selflessly cut his cloak in half to share it with him. He eventually became a bishop and a saint, honored each year on Saint Martin's Day, the 11th of November.

This time of year also coincides with the end of the harvest period, and historically, this date served as the deadline for farmers to make their rental payments. Therefore, the timing was perfect for a celebration with family and friends. Traditionally, a pig was slaughtered for the occasion. The farmers preserved some of the meat for winter, but they also had an abundance of pork to share—a luxury not frequently enjoyed. During the feast, every part of the pig was used—a true nose-to-tail dining experience.

Today, the Swiss Department of Home Affairs recognizes the Feast of Saint Martin as a *tradition vivante* ('living tradition'). However, as it mentions in the description of this event, the current version of Saint Martin "is more about celebrating the pig than the holy man."

While the Feast of Saint Martin remains the main event of the festivities, in recent decades, Porrentruy has also started hosting a special outdoor market featuring regional food products, live entertainment and more. In this town, the celebration of Saint Martin is typically held the second weekend of November. Although, if the first of November falls on a Sunday, the celebration takes place the third weekend of the month.

During this time of year, restaurants in the Porrentruy area, and elsewhere in the Jura, will offer a traditional menu. The menu varies, but to be considered an official partner of the event, a restaurant must agree to serve at least one of the following dishes: (1) *gelée* (also known as *gelée de ménage*), a terrine made with pig's head meat encased in a savory meat jelly; (2) *boudin*, a blood sausage made with pork and cream, or (3) grillades, grilled pork sausages, and *atriaux*, a round sausage made with pork meat and liver with a lacy *crépine* (caul fat) casing.

If you go all in for the feast of Saint. Martin with a *menu complet*, you can expect about 8-12 different courses. If you eat the traditional mid-day meal, it is estimated that you will consume between 3000 and 4000 calories! About halfway through this extensive meal, you might also be invited to have a *coup de milieu*—a small glass of damassine, a regional eau-de-vie made from plums, or another fruit brandy. In more recent years, the damasson rouge plum has been used to make a light, refreshing sorbet.

Damassine AOP *(appellation d'origine protégée)*, is an eau-de-vie made with the *damasson rouge* plum. This eau-de-vie has a long history in the Jura, which led to it earning an *appellation d'origine protégée* (AOP) designation in 2010. In order to obtain the AOP label, this alcoholic beverage must be produced in the Jura with local ingredients. Before this designation, people referred to these plums as Damassine, but now this name only technically applies to the beverage.

Harvested by hand, generally between mid-July and the end of September, these delicate little violet-red plums are then put into barrels. After a period of fermentation, the distilling process takes place, and no later than December 31 of the year of their harvest. Producers cannot sell Damassine AOP until November 11, the day of Saint Martin of the year following the harvest.

The Swiss typically consume Damassine AOP as a digestif after a meal. Ideally, you serve this clear drink in a stemmed, fluted glass. When you taste it, you immediately notice the distinct sweet smell and taste of these special plums.

Combining fresh plums with a splash of Damassine AOP (or another fruit brandy), with a hint of rosemary and honey, this sorbet makes for a refreshing dessert after a heavy meal—whether for the Feast of Saint Martin or after a cheese fondue.

Finally, if you want to learn more about these special plums, you should visit Ô Vergers d'Ajoie. Located just outside the city of Porrentruy, this agritourism site opened in 2018 and has several different functions. It serves as Switzerland's museum of fruit and distillation, as well as a center of information for Damassine AOP.

VII

ACKNOWLEDGEMENTS
DANK
REMERCIEMENTS

VII. ACKNOWLEDGEMENTS

Thank you first and foremost to my family—my husband Nate and our two sons, Augustus and Hendrik. As always, they represent my first and most effective food critics! We have had so much fun testing and retesting all of these sweet and Swiss recipes.

Once again, it was an absolute pleasure to work with the team at Helvetiq to prepare this book. I am grateful for their support, and especially for the unwavering enthusiasm of Hadi Barkat, the eagle-eye edits from Satu Binggeli and the amazing layout and illustrations from Ajša Zdravković.

The outstanding photographs in this book come from the tremendously talented photographer Dorian Rollin, in partnership with my favorite food stylist Camille Stoos. I had so much fun working with them. Their attention to detail and sense of humor make them an invaluable team. We ate a lot of desserts during our photo shoot! So much so that we had a good laugh late in the week when Camille's button burst off the waist of her pants (likely just a funny coincidence, or the result of too many slices of chocolate cake!).

A big thanks to the following chefs for trusting me with their recipes: Romano Hasenauer of Auberge du Chalet-des-Enfants (Le Mont-sur-Lausanne), Zineb Hattab of Restaurant KLE (Zürich), Bernadette Lisibach of Neue Blumenau (Lömmenschwil), Torsten Rönisch of Hotel Restaurant Capricorns (Wergenstein) and Arthur Sartore of Grotto Due Ponti (Giornico). Given all their other responsibilities, they generously made the time to talk with me and shared their recipes. I have very good memories of dining at each of their restaurants, and I am so happy to include their stories in this book. Please visit their restaurants, when you can.

To all the people who generously agreed to test my recipes, I am so truly thankful for your helpful feedback: Inga Aellen, Kate Allen, David Anchel, Susannah Bloch, Kate Blumenreich, Rain Caldes, Madhu Capelli, Claire Fitzpatrick, funambuline, Laura Elena Gómez, Mylène Jeanneret, Louise Kasser Genecand, Kelly Kratzer & Elsa Rezac, Jeana & Zach Marshak, Laura Monfrooe, Stephen & Amantha Moore, Nathan Moore, Laure Niquille Rahman, Susan Renna, Jennifer Robertson, Molly Schuetze, Brigitte Streiff and Julie Walder.

I also really appreciate the time the following people took to review sections of the book: Olivier & Géraldine Boillat, Salina Swanson, Sherly Cho, Sarah Kohler, Philippe Martin, Francesca Martini, Nathan Moore, Ludovic Moulin, Melayna Nieuwsma, Mara Nieuwsma, Jörg Widmer and Nancy Wolf.

Finally, I would like to recognize the in-kind support of the Stiftung Ferien im Baudenkmal. They allowed us to take the photographs for this book at their vacation apartment in the Schlossgut Münchenwiler. You will see architectural elements from this property in the background of many photos in this book. We partnered with this foundation for my first book, and I am indebted to them for allowing us to use one of

their properties again for this book.
The Stiftung Ferien im Baudenkmal is committed to the preservation of historic properties, such as the Schlossgut Münchenwiler, throughout Switzerland. Oftentimes, it helps to save heritage sites that would have otherwise been lost. In turn, these properties become available to the public as one-of-a-kind vacation homes and apartments. It gives Swiss residents and tourists alike the unique chance to experience one of these historically significant sites firsthand as a temporary resident.

A former manor house, Schlossgut Münchenwiler is located on a small piece of land that belongs to the canton of Bern and is surrounded on all sides by the canton of Fribourg. The eastern part of the property, in which the Schlossgut Münchenwiler apartment is located, dates from the 17th century and served as a cheese dairy and residential building. Today this apartment has two bedrooms for up to four people. Another apartment with nearly the same layout upstairs is also available for rental. Once again, the opportunity for us to use such a historic site for our photo shoot is an experience that I will never forget.

FOR MORE INFORMATION

Stiftung Ferien im Baudenkmal
Zollikerstrasse 128
8008 Zürich
+41 (0)44 252 28 72
info@fib.ch
ferienimbaudenkmal.ch

INDEX

RECIPES BY GEOGRAPHIC AREAS

Here is a list of the recipes in this book by what is generally considered their place of origin or the epicenter of their production in Switzerland. Some of these recipes may carry a different name, depending on the linguistic region.

THROUGHOUT SWITZERLAND

- Brönnti Crème, p. 187
- Carac, p. 123 (although strongly associated with Suisse Romande)
- Einback / Zwieback, p. 27
- Meringues (Bern, Fribourg and Vaud), p. 213
- Nussgipfel, p. 39
- Chocolate Gugelhopf, p. 95
- Spitzbuben, p. 173

THURGAU / ST. GALLEN

- Apple Meringue with Süssmostcreme, Rum Raisin Ice Cream and Hüppen, p. 199

TICINO

- Ciambelle, p. 153
- Crèfli, p. 157
- Pane dei morti, p. 73
- Torta di pane, p. 83

VAUD

- Salée ormonanche, p. 53
- Tarte à la raisinée, p. 137

VALAIS

- Apricot Jalousien, p. 65
- Flon de Savièse, p. 115
- Heiperchochchüechu, p. 209

ZUG

- Griessauflauf with Cherries, p. 195

A list of sources can be found on Heddi's blog
https://cuisinehelvetica.com

Sweet + Swiss
Delicious and Easy Desserts from the Heart of Europe

Author: Heddi Nieuwsma
Graphic Design & Illustrations: Ajša Zdravković, Elżbieta Kownacka
Photography: Dorian Rollin
Food Styling: Camille Stoos
Proofreading: Chad Jorgenson

Photo credit:
84: Grotto dei Due Ponti
87, 139: Heddi Nieuwsma
106, 107: Restaurant KLE

ISBN: 978-3-907293-68-3
First edition: September 2022
Deposit copy in Switzerland: September 2022
Printed in the Czech Republic

Avenue des Acacias 7
CH-1006 Lausanne, Switzerland

helvetiq.com